The Military & Hospitaller Order of St Lazarus of Jerusalem

The Office of the Grand Hospitaller

A historical review

H.E. Chev. Charles Savona-Ventura

Published by: Lulu Press Inc, 627 Davis Drive, Suite 300, Morrisville, NC 27560
ISBN: 978-1-4717-1156-5

Contents

Introduction

The Order of St Lazarus saw its origins in the early fifth century as an establishment located outside the walls of Jerusalem serving the needs of victims of leprosy. The establishment became a formal monastic hospitaller order after the First Crusade of 1099. This hospitaller function persisted through the 12-13th centuries expanding its role throughout Christian Europe. The statutes of the Order during this period mentions that in the *monastery of Jerusalem, there shall be fifty-two sick confrères and, in addition to these, one should admit at least as many sick people as the number of spaces left by the confrères. …. They shall be given gowns and food from the House until their death.* [1]

Lazarite brethren caring for the lepers in the Jerusalem leprosarium

---

[1] Savona-Ventura, Charles [editor]. Die Regül deß Heiligen Ordens S. Lazari 1314/1321 zu 1418 -The Rules of the Holy Order of S. Lazarus 1314/1321 to 1418. Sancti Lazari Ordinis Academia Internationalis, Malta, 2019, p.108.

The 14th century Black Death epidemics saw an apparent overall decline in the number of lepers. Together with a changing attitude towards the social position imposed on lepers within the community they lived in, this apparent decline in prevalence led to a decrease in the number of leprosaria institutions needed. In England, St Giles leprosarium at Holborn housed 40 inmates when transferred to the Order's management in 1299. By 1345, the staff of eight carers were catering for 14 lepers, and by 1402 were catering for only four victims. However, the hospitaller activities expanded to outside the leprosaria supporting lepers in the community. In 1479 at Burton Lazars in England, the establishment was obliged to support 14 lepers who if not institutionalized were supported by paying *them a weekly sum of money for the necessities of life*. [2]

The political turmoil of the 16th century saw the Order split up into regional components with distinct loyalties to the local rulers. It also gradually assumed a more military role to become, by the end of the 16th century, an honorific order of chivalry awarded for services rendered to the French king. However, the hospitaller role was maintained even during these tremulous centuries. An attempt was made by the French king in 1672 to strengthen to hospitaller function of the Order and place all the hospitals in the realm under the Order's management. A 1690 report of the income accruing from the holdings of the Order in France lists a significant number of hospitaller establishments – *maladeries, hôpitaux, and maison/ hôtel-*

---

[2] Marcombe, David. Leper Knights - The Order of St Lazarus of Jerusalem in England, c.1150-1544. Boydell Press, Suffolk – England, 2003, p.135-174

Dieu.[3] The 1672 Royal Edict was repealed in 1693, but in spite of loosing many of the newly acquired hospital-related benefices, the Order still held on to its originally owned ones.

The French Revolution put philanthropy on the backburner. However, following the Bourbon restoration and the loss of Royal protection in 1830, the French Order assumed a new hospitaller role of supporting philanthropic activities in the Holy Land. In the mid-19th century, the Order of Saint Lazarus is documented as supporting the re-building of the Monastery of Mount Carmel at Haifa.[4]

Mount Carmel Stella Maris Monastery in Haifa, Israel, 1875
© Anonymous

---

[3] Le Pelletier, Jacques. Recueil général de tous les bénéfices & Commanderies de France, & de ses dépendances. Le Pelletier, Paris, 1690, Section 5.
[4] Alexander Dumas, Adolphe Dumas. Temple et Hospice du Mont-Carmel en Palesine. Fain & Thunot, Paris, 1844, pp.11-12.

This raison d'être was eventually entrenched in the 1910 statutes – *the Hospitaller knights shall fulfil their mission. When possible, and without obligation to their conscience, and piously give their person to the service of the Church, to the poor, the lepers and other sick persons, and to travellers and pilgrims. … Patriarchal authority assures that the gifts are distributed among their hospices, missions and works for the greater glory of the Holy Church, evangelization of the infidel, and the solace of the poor and sick.*[5] In the late 1920s, the philanthropic link with the Melkite Patriarchy was emphasized in communication involving the setting up of the Grand Bailiwick of the Order of Saint Lazarus of Jerusalem in the United States of Mexico. In that communication from the Grand Aumônier of the Order representing H.B. Cyril IX to the Marquis of Guadalupe Carlos Rincón-Gallardo y Romero de Terreros, reference was made to assisting the missionary and hospital work of the Greek Melchite Catholic Patriarchate: *I have the firm hope that Your Excellency will do well to contribute to the development in his country of this chivalrous order which devotes its activity to supporting and assisting the missionary and hospital work of the Greek Melchite Catholic Patriarchate.*[6]

During the Second World War, the Order suffered a serious setback in its internationalization drive and caused it to concentrate its main efforts

---

[5] de Jandriac. Les chevaliers Hospitaliers de Saint Lazare de Jerusalem et de Notre Dame de la Merci. Rivista Araldica, November 1913, XI(11):pp.679-683.

[6] Letter Archimandrite representing the Melkite Patriarch H.B. Cyril IX to the Marquis of Guadalupe, undated but c.1930. *Documents belonging to Coutant de Sasseval (former Chancellor, Paris Obedience) relating to Mexico.* Originally Canadian Box 7/9[6m] transferred to Pre-1960 Archives Box, Torri ta' Lanzun Archives – MHOSLJ, Malta.

on the national front, particularly in the occupied French territories providing volunteer emergency ambulance and personnel services.[7]

Presentation of the Anglo-American Ambulance Corps of Cannes
Villa Montfleury, 5th February 1940
© Historical Committee of the Hospitallers of Saint-Lazare.[8]

In the aftermath of the Second World War, the Order increasingly expanded its activities to an unlimited scope of philanthropy with an international worldwide perspective especially in France and Spain. In the immediate post-war period, the Order set up the Dispensary of St Lazarus

[7] Savona-Ventura, Charles. The WWII war effort of the Order of Saint Lazarus. Grand Priory of the Maltese Islands – MHOSLJ, Malta, 2021, +64pp.

[8] *http://expos-historiques.cannes.com/a/3522/l-anglo-american-ambulance-corps-de-cannes-fevrier-1940-traverso-13fi190-/*

in Paris (1945) and had a share of the Surgical Ward at St Joseph Hospital in Paris (1945). In Spain, the Order also undertook several philanthropic hospitaller initiatives mainly related to leprosy. As a result of these activities in Spain, General Francisco Franco, in 1946, confirmed the previous official recognition of the Order given in 1940 by the Spanish Ministry of the Interior of the Order which associated the Order with the national fight against leprosy, skin disorders and sexual transmitted diseases.[9]

The Order further aided the families of victims of leprosy in the Spanish State. In 1948, it organized an exhibition to promote the fight against leprosy and participated in the Health Exhibition held in Madrid in 1957. Foreign jurisdiction sent medicines and gifts for the treatment of lepers in Spain (1951/53), and in 1952 assisted the Spanish leprosaria of Trillo Chapineria [established in December 1943 – closed in 1996] and the Sanatorium of San Francisco de Borja (often referred to as Fontilles) in Vall de Laguart [est. 1909].[10]

---

[9] *Orden Hospitalaria de San Lazaro de Jerusalen*. Order dated 9 May 1940 from the Ministry of the Interior, Spain; and *Articulo 22/25; Decreto de 8 de marzo de 1946 por el que se aprueba el Reglamento par la lucha contra la Lepra, Dermatosis y Enfermedades sexuales*. Vide: Jaime Nuno de Montells y Pajares. *Ordo Sancti Lazari Repertorio Bibliografico/Bibliography 1930-2005*. Grand Priory of Spain, MHOSLJ – Madrid, 2005, p.57-59.

[10] L'Oeuvre charitable de l'Ordre de Saint Lazare de Jerusalem. *La Croix de Sinople – The Green Cross*, 1965, 1(3/4):pp.45-47.

El sanatorio de Fontilles

By the mid-1960s, the Order was outreaching to different continents with projects directed at helping the victims of leprosy, including: [11]

- MIDDLE EAST
  - The Order supported the foundation of a "Saint Lazarus Ward" at the Hospital of the Mission de la Vallée des Chrétiens de Salifa, Syria, managed by the Greek Catholic Melchite Missionaries of Saint Paul (1960-1963).

- AFRICA
  - The Order provided gifts and subsidies to the Committee of Assistance to support Africans sick with leprosy.

---

[11] *La Croix de Sinople – The Green Cross*, 1965, 1(3/4):pp.45-47.

o   It further gave help and assistance to the Leper-house of the Holy Angels at Ouidah in the Republic of Dahomey (1963).

- THAILAND
  - o   The Order gave patronage to the Protestant Hospital of North Thailand (1963) and to the leper clinic and settlements of the Redemptorist Fathers' Mission in Thailand providing care for 1500 lepers at Khon Kaen (1964).
  - o   It further provided drugs and medicines for the leper-houses in the Kingdom of Thailand (1 ton of medicines in 1963, valued at GB£27,000 or US$75,000).
  - o   It also gave toys to the children of leper settlements in the Kingdom of Thailand (1963).

Chiangmai Leprosy Colony, founded by James McKean in 1908
© McKean Rehabilitation Centre

- U.S.A.
    - The Order provided wireless sets for the use of the lepers at the Hospital of the Committee of Los Angeles, U.S.A.

- EUROPE
    - The Order set up a Leprosy Commission and a Leprosy Research Fund in the countries of the English Tongue bringing together the world's principal English-speaking leprologists to study medical techniques to counter leprosy (1963).[12]
    - It further organized charitable functions in Scotland, England, Thailand, Australia, and Nigeria in aid of lepers (1963).[13]

---

[12] The eradication of leprosy. Green Cross Booklets, January 1964, 3:+12pp.
[13] Report on the Charitable Work of the English tongue. Green Cross Booklets, November 1964, 5:+7pp.

In addition, other non-leprosy directed philanthropic activities included:

- Supporting Repatriation Schemes of orphans and victims of the catastrophe caused by the flooding of Fréjus, the result of dam failure in November 1959.
- Providing gifts of food and presents to poor Indians in the Indian reserve in the State of Utah, U.S.A. [14]

---

[14] *La Croix de Sinople – The Green Cross*, 1965, 1(3/4):pp.45-47.

The Office of the Grand Hospitaller

While the primary function of the Order of Saint Lazarus had always been a hospitaller one particularly targeting the care of the victims of leprosy, the office of Hospitaller was first introduced as part of the administration structure of the Grand Bailiwick General of the British Realms and the Commissionerate of the Lands of the English Tongue and South Africa by decree dated 25th October 1963. [15] This office however only applied to the budding English Tongue management structure.

Establishing the Office

The Office of the Grand Hospitaller within the general administrative structure of the International Order was only first mentioned in the 1968 draft revision of the Order's statute: *Le Grand Magistère de l'Ordre peut, s'il le juge opportune, désigner un Grand Hospitalier de l'Ordre qui a pour mission, sous la direction du Gouvernement Central se l'Ordre, de contrôller l'action hospitalière de l'Ordre et de coordonner ses oeuvres charitables.*[16]

---

[15] Statutes, Regulations and Commands governing the Order in the Grand Bailiwick General in the British Realms….. Green Cross Booklets, April 1965, 6:17.

[16] '*The Grand Magistery of the Order may, if it deems appropriate, designate a Grand Hospitaller of the Order whose mission, under the direction of the Central Government of the Order, is to oversee the hospitaller actions of the Order and to coordinate its charitable works.*' See: MHOSLJ.

These draft statutes however did not envisaged appointing a regular dedicated officer to the post of Grand Hospitaller, but only appointed one if the Grand Magistery deemed it appropriate.

The Office was only formally set up within the Order's organizational structure in 1969 with the promulgation of the Grand Magistral decree 08/69 which introduced statutory changes restructuring the Grand Chancery composition to include several officials including the appointed grand hospitaller. The first appointee to the post, made on the 15th April 1969, was H.E. Chev. Prof. Charles Connor O'Malley BSc, MB., DOMS, GCM, GCLJ. Decree 39/69 also obliged each jurisdiction to submit a full annual hospitaller report to the Grand Chancery.[17] The role of the Grand Hospitaller remained vaguely defined as being that of overseeing the philanthropic activities of the Order.[18]

In 1992, the meeting of the Grand Magistral Council held in Spain approved '*the creation of a Hospitaller Committee to establish the various medical needs afforded at the present, to identify new areas of special needs, and to correlate the*

Règles, Statuts et Coutumes de l'Ordre de Saint-Lazare de Jèrusalem. La Vie Chevaleresque, 1968, N.S. 4:p.11.

[17] MHOSLJ. Constitutional decrees 46th Grand Master H.R.H. Prince Charles Philip of Orleans, Duke of Nemours, Vendome, and Alençon. MHOSLJ, Delft – The Netherlands, 1969, pp.4, 14, 29.

[18] MHOSLJ. Constitution, Statutes and Regulations of the Order of St. Lazarus of Jerusalem - Malta Obedience: Magistral Decree No. 17 /99, 1999.

whole work of the Order in one report.[19] No action appears to have been taken at this time to implement this proposal.

The 2006 Joint Reunification Commission drew up a review draft of the Order's Constitution and Byelaws. In the reviewed constitution, Article 9.1.6 deals specifically with the office of the Grand Hospitaller stating that: *The Grand Hospitaller shall be the senior medical officer of the Order and shall be responsible for advising the Grand Master, the Grand Magistral Council and the national jurisdictions of, and consulting with them on, the hospitaller activities of the Order.* [20]

The reviewed byelaws also saw the setting up of the Hospitaller Standing Commission as one of the two Standing Commissions of the Order (the other being the Ecumenical Commission). Art. 6.2: *The Commission will consist of all Jurisdictional Hospitallers and headed by the Grand Hospitaller, ex-officio. It will meet at the call of the Grand Hospitaller but in no case less frequently than at each Grand Magistral Council meeting. The Hospitaller Committee shall serve as the principal forum for planning, recommending, implementing and evaluating the Hospitaller activities of the National Jurisdictions of the Order and of the Order as a whole. Each Jurisdiction will be represented by its Hospitaller or his*

---

[19] MHOSLJ. The Military and Hospitaller Order of Saint Lazarus of Jerusalem - Report of the Grand Magistral Council Castle of Albatarrec, Lerida, Spain 14th to 18th May 1992. MHOSLJ, 1992, p.69.

[20] MHOSLJ. The Constitution of the Military and Hospitaller Order of Saint Lazarus of Jerusalem. Agreed by the Joint Reunification Commission, Toronto 18 February 2006/Amended 11 March 2006, p.6.

or her representative approved by the Grand Hospitaller. [21] The Hospitaller Commission was formally established by a Grand Magistral Council Resolution on the 18th November 2016. The resolution resolved that the Commission was authorized *to do and perform any and all such acts, including execution of any and all documents and certificates, as such members shall deem necessary or advisable.* [22]

In addition, the 2006 byelaws further defined the duties of the jurisdictional hospitallers: Art. 6.3 *The Head of each Jurisdiction of the Order, in consultation with the Grand Hospitaller, will appoint a member of the Jurisdiction who is a health professional or a suitably qualified alternative as his Jurisdictional Hospitaller. The Jurisdictional Hospitaller shall be responsible for the overall planning (strategic and tactical), recommending, implementing, and evaluating the Hospitaller activities of the Jurisdiction in conjunction with the Jurisdictional Head and in harmony with the overall strategic and tactical goals of the Order. The Jurisdictional Hospitaller will report to the Head of Jurisdiction concerning day-to-day operations. The Jurisdictional Hospitaller or his approved representative approved by the Grand Hospitaller will attend all meetings of the Hospitaller Commission and actively participate in all communications with the Grand Hospitaller including providing an annual report detailing the Hospitaller activities of the National Jurisdiction.* [23] These

---

[21] MHOSLJ. The By-Laws of the MHOSLJ. Agreed by the Joint Reunification Commission, Toronto 24 September 2006, p.11.

[22] MHOSLJ. Grand Magistral Council Resolution 18 November 2016: Resolution to confirm the Establishment of the Hospitaller Commission.

[23] MHOSLJ. The By-Laws of the MHOSLJ. Agreed by the Joint Reunification Commission, Toronto 24 September 2006, p.11.

statutory articles have been virtually retained in the updated 2018 review of the byelaws.[24]

The job description of the Office of the Grand Hospitaller and the Hospitaller Commission remained vague. An attempt to collate and define these was made in 2013. These were published in the International Grand Hospitaller Report for that year.[25]

---

[24] MHOSLJ. The By-Laws of the Order. Agreed by the GMC, 3 November 2018, p.19.
[25] Mittelstaedt, Axel. The Military and Hospitaller Order of St. Lazarus of Jerusalem. International 2013 Hospitaller Report. MHOSLJ, 2014, pp.34-35

JOB DESCRIPTION GRAND HOSPITALLER

Constitutional Job Summary

In accordance with Article 9.1.6 of the Constitution, the Grand Hospitaller shall be the senior medical officer of the Order and shall be responsible for advising the Grand Master, the Grand Magistral Council and the jurisdictions of, and consulting with them on, the hospitaller activities of the Order.

Position in the Order

The Grand Hospitaller is a member of the Grand Executive Committee (GEC). He/ she is one Principal Grand Officers of the Order reporting to the Grand Commander.

Appointment & Term of Appointment

The Grand Hospitaller is appointed by the Grand Master. He/ she is appointed for a period of three years, which can be extended for a period or periods not exceeding 10 years in total.

Upon the discretion of the Grand Master he/ she can be given the dignity of a Grand Hospitaller Emeritus by the Chapter General or, if it is not convened at the time the Grand Hospitaller resigns from office, by the Grand Master in consultation with the Grand Magistral Council.

As a (Principal) Grand Officer he/ she is not allowed to hold the position of a Head, Deputy Head and/ or Chancellor of a National Jurisdiction or another (additional) position as a (Principal)Grand Officer.

Qualifications for the Office

The Grand Hospitaller must be a suitably qualified health professional preferably as a physician. He must be familiar with the secular humanitarian mission of the Order and must have proven experience in operating in a multi-national environment as well as in working together with different governmental and non-governmental health or charity organizations. He/ she must have served the Order as a Grand Officer, preferably as Vice Grand Hospitaller, Head of a National Jurisdiction or Hereditary Commander prior to being appointed as Grand Hospitaller for at least a term of three years. He/ she must hold at least the rank of a Knight (KLJ) or Dame (DLJ) of the Order

Primary Duties & Responsibilities

The Grand Hospitaller:
- is the chairperson of the Hospitaller Commission and ensures that the Hospitaller Commission will meet in no case less frequently than the Grand Magistral Council.
- is responsible for issuing guidelines on effective hospitaller work of the Order and its jurisdictions
- is responsible for the coordination of hospitaller and charitable work and projects of the jurisdictions including those of the Grand and Hereditary Commanderies
- is responsible for managing the hospitaller and charitable activities of the international Order and the integration of matching jurisdictional activities into those.
- is responsible for ensuring that national hospitallers are adequately qualified
- provides advice and counsel to the Grand Master and the Grand Executive Committee and, in co-operation with the Vice-Grand Hospitaller, to the Grand Magistral Council and jurisdictions of the Order
- prepares and publishes via the communication division an annual hospitaller report of the Order
- to involve the Vice Grand Hospitaller in the affairs of this office in such a manner that the Vice Grand Hospitaller is able to assume the responsibilities on short notice

Primary Competencies

The Grand Hospitaller has the competence and authority:
- to chair the Hospitaller Commission of the Order
- to propose a suitable candidate for the position of Vice Grand Hospitaller
- to approve all candidates for the position of a jurisdictional hospitaller
- to dismiss a national Hospitaller from the Hospitaller Commission on serious reason given after consultation with the Grand Commander and the respective Head of Jurisdiction
- to request an annual hospitaller report via the Vice-Grand Chancellors Administration and Finance
- to issue guidelines and directives developed within his division throughout the Order with the approval of the Grand Executive Committee
- to set the agenda for the Hospitaller Commission meetings after consultation with the Vice Grand Hospitaller

Council & Committee Membership

The Grand Hospitaller is, as a Principal Grand Officer and/ or ex-officio a member of:
- the Grand Executive Committee
- the Grand Magistral Council
- the Hospitaller Commission
- the Heads of Jurisdiction Meeting in attendance

Reporting

The Grand Hospitaller reports to the
- Grand Commander
- Grand Executive Committee

Substitution

The Grand Hospitaller is substituted by the Vice Grand Hospitaller

In 2011, a Grand Hospitaller Board was set up *to ensure a direct personal contact, a continuous information flow and regular communication to the jurisdictional hospitallers of a specific region in our globalised world. In addition, this structure supports motivation for joint activities and expert assistance by bundling different and specific knowledge as well as professional experiences.* This board however only survived a couple of years. The appointed board was made up of the following members.[26]

Chairperson ex ufficio	H.E. Chev. Dr.med. Axel Mittlestaedt, GCLJ, GCMLJ, GCrLJ - Grand Hospitaller
The Americas	Chev. John Byrnes, Jr., KLJ, GMLJ, BrCRLJ – Grand Prioral Hospitaller for America
Europe	Dame Dr. Heather Payne, MBBS, DCH, FRCPCH, DLJ, - Grand Prioral Hospitaller for England and Wales
	Chev. Dr.med. Juan-Evangelists Ruiz de Burgos Moreno KLJ(J). Prioral Hospitaller for Spain
Oceania-Australia	Chev. Rex Morgan, AM, MBE, KLJ, Prioral Hospitaller for Australia
Africa	No nomination

Incumbents to the Post of Grand Hospitaller

The first person appointed to the post of Grand Hospitaller in 1969 was Prof. Charles Connor O'Malley. Over these past five decades, there have been seven other incumbents in the post. These officers have all been highly qualified professionals in the field of medicine and have all used their medical expertise and experience to promote and strengthen, in whatever way they could, the philanthropic facet of the Order and develop the role of the Office of the Grand Hospitaller as entrenched in the Order's Constitution.

---

[26] Mittelstaedt, Axel. The Military and Hospitaller Order of St. Lazarus of Jerusalem. International 2011 Hospitaller Report. MHOSLJ, 2012

List of Grand Hospitallers	
• Prof. Charles Connor O'Malley:	1969-1982
• Dr. Hans von Leden	: 1980-1988
• Prof. Luis Dolcet Buxeres	: 1988-1994
• Dr. Jaime Cremona	: 1994-1998
• Dr. Kenneth Paul Moritsugu	: 1998-2012
• Dr. Axel Mittelstaedt	: 2012-2015
• Prof. Brett Delahunt	: 2015-2021
• Prof. Charles Savona-Ventura	: 2021 et sec

Prof. Charles Connor O'Malley GCLJ (1889-1982) qualified B.Sc. in anatomy and physiology (1914) and M.B. (1917) from the University College Galway, Ireland. He continued his post-graduate studies in several London hospitals and obtained further qualifications including a M.D., M.Ch., and Diploma in Ophthalmic Medicine and Surgery. His professional speciality was as an Ear, Nose, and Throat (ENT) surgeon and Ophthalmologist, being eventually appointed consultant ophthalmologist and otologist to the Galway Central Hospital (1930–65) and Professor of Ophthalmology and Otology at University College Galway (1931–59). In 1917, he volunteered for the Royal Navy medical service, and saw action at sea as surgeon-lieutenant aboard the

23

aircraft carrier HMS Furious and served briefly as a captain in the RAF. O'Malley became a member of the Sovereign Military Order of Malta when, in 1938, he set up the Order of Malta ambulance corps in Ireland. He was made a knight grand cross of the Order of Malta in 1946. He joined the Military and Hospitaller Order of Saint Lazarus of Jerusalem [MHOSLJ] when the Bailiwick of Ireland was inaugurated in 1962 serving as the referendary to the bailiwick [GC No. 0146]. He was in 1969 appointed to the newly created post of Grand Hospitaller to serve the Order on the Grand Magistral Council. Prof. O'Malley died aged 93 years after a long illness on 22nd July 1982.[27]

Dr. Hans Victor von Leden GCLJ (1918-2014) qualified M.D. (1941) and Sc.D. from Loyola University in Chicago, U.S.A. He further specialized in otolaryngology and plastic surgery at the Mayo Clinic in Rochester, Minnesota and eventually worked as an ENT specialist in Chicago. In 1961, he was appointed Professor of Otolaryngology at University of California, Los Angeles (UCLA) Medical School and established the Institute of Laryngology and Voice Disorders. In 1966, he assumed the Chair of Biocommunication at the University of Southern California in Los

[27] Foley, Aideen. O'Malley, (Charles) Conor. In: Dictionary of Irish Biography. Dublin, Royal Irish Academy, 2022, available https://www.dib.ie/biography/omalley-charles-conor-a6883

Angeles, retiring in 1985. He was the recipient of multiple national and international awards for contributions to medicine and science, and had received decorations from the United States, the Holy See, Germany, Spain, Italy, Switzerland, Portugal, Mexico, New Zealand, among others. He joined the MHOSLJ in 1970 [GC No. 0601] to eventually be appointed Grand Prior of the American jurisdiction. In 1980, he was appointed in the conjoint Grand Hospitaller post to support Prof. O'Malley, taking over the role completely after the latter's death in 1982. He occupied the post up to 1988. Dr. von Leden died aged 95 years on 5th March 2014. [28]

Prof. Luis Dolcet Buxeres GCLJ (collar) (1909-1994) qualified as a medical doctor and specialized in Ophthalmology, receiving a doctorate from the University of Madrid. He dedicated himself fully to the specialty at the Vall d'Hebron Hospital in Barcelona, where he became the Head of the Ophthalmology Service and contributed to the teaching of the speciality at the Autonomous University of Barcelona. He joined the MHOSLJ in 1976 [GC No. 2058] and was appointed to the

[28] Wendler, Jurgen. Prof. Hans Victor von Leden. Union of the European Phoniatricians, 2014, available https://www.uep.phoniatrics.eu/membership/obituary/prof-hans-victor-von-leden/index.html

post of Grand Hospitaller in 1988, remaining in office until his death in 1994. Prof. Dolcet Buxeres died aged 84 years on 21st January 1994.[29]

Dr. Jaime Cremona GCLJ, KMLJ, SCrLJ (1936---) qualified as a medical doctor receiving an M.D. from the Royal University of Malta in 1967 and subsequently specialized in the field of obstetrics and gynaecology in the UK obtaining fellowships of various professional associations such as FICS, FACS, and FRCOG. After serving the Maltese community, he transferred to Saudi Arabia in 1979 where he served as the consulting obstetrics-gynaecologist to the royal family there. Returning to Malta, he joined the MHOSLJ in 1993 [GC No. 3511] being appointed Grand Prior of the Maltese Islands and eventually was asked to serve on the Supreme Council in the role of Grand Hospitaller and Vice-Chancellor & Secretary General. He resigned his posts in 1997 to take over as President of the Malta Association of the Sovereign Order of St. John. He currently serves as Patron of the affiliate voluntary organization of the MHOSLJ Grand Priory of the Maltese Islands, the Raoul Follereau Foundation [Malta] – Order of Charity.

---

[29] Académicos de nuestra historia centenaria: Luis Dolcet Buxeres. Real Academia Europea de Doctores-Barcelona 1914 (RAED), December 11, 2019, https://raed.academy/academicos-de-nuestra-historia-centenaria-luis-dolcet-buxeres/

Dr. Kenneth Paul Moritsugu (1945---) received his bachelor's degree from the University of Hawaii (1967), an M.D. from the George Washington University School of Medicine (1971), and a Master of Public Health (Health Administration and Planning) from the UC Berkeley School of Public Health (1975). He has had a long career as a physician and public health administrator. He served as a rear admiral in the United States Public Health Service Commissioned Corps and in 1998 was appointed to the post of Deputy Surgeon General and acting Surgeon General in 2006, retiring in 2007. He has received multiple awards and decorations from the U.S. Public Health Service, the Federal Bureau of Prisons, the United States Army, the Department of Defence, and the United States Coast Guard. He joined the MHOSLJ and was appointed Grand Hospitaller in 1998 holding the office until 2012, publishing during his tenure the first of the subsequent series of annual international hospitaller reports in 2010. He currently serves as the Hospitaller Ambassador of the Order of Saint Lazarus.[30]

---

[30] Kenneth P. Moritsugu. In: Wikipedia, the free encyclopedia, U.S.A., 2021, https://en.wikipedia.org/wiki/Kenneth_P._Moritsugu; Saint Lazarus Newsletter, January 2004, 22:pp.10-11,

Dr. Axel Mittelstaedt GCLJ, GCMLJ, GCrLJ. He qualified as a medical doctor and specialized in internal medicine (internist). In 1979, he was appointed head of Internal Medicine at the Augusta-Ktankenhaus in Dusseldorf, Germany and eventually served as associate board members of the management team of the hospital. He joined the MHOSLJ and was eventually appointed Grand Prior of the Romanian jurisdiction being awarded the status of Grand Prior emeritus in 2009 [GM Decree 03/09]. In 2010, he was appointed a member of the Governance Working Group [GM decree 49/10] to serve as the deputy Grand Magistral Delegate for European Affairs [GM decree 18/10] assuming the role as Grand Magistral Delegate in 2011 [GM decree 26/11]. He assumed the role of Grand Hospitaller in 2012 serving until 2015. He currently serves as Grand Hospitaller Emeritus.

Prof. Brett Delahunt ONZM, KStJ, GCLJ GCMLJ GCrLJ GMLJ (1950---) received his BSc(Hons) from Victoria University of Wellington (1972), completed a BMedSc (1976), MB ChB (1978) and MD by research (1995) from the University of Otago. He specialised in the field of pathology with special reference to urological pathology being subsequently admitted as fellow to relevant professional colleges – the Australasia Royal College of Pathologists (1985), the London, U.K. Royal College of Pathologists (2005), and the New Zealand Society of Pathologists (2012). In 1980, he joined the clinical staff of the Wellington Hospital/Capital & Coast DHB and the academic staff of the Wellington School of Medicine and Health Sciences, University of Otago moving up the scale to be appointed Professor of Pathology in 1996. He has served on multiple professional boards and on editorial boards of a number of professional journals. Over his professional career, he has received a significant number of awards and distinctions. He has been awarded a number of professional awards including membership to the Order of Saint John (OStJ, 1986; CStJ, 1993; KStJ, 1995), being made an Officer of the New Zealand Order of Merit (ONZM) for services to pathology (2004) and being appointed an Officer of the Royal Order of Arts and Sciences (Royal Order of Moniseraphon) of Cambodia in 2006 and Commander of the Order of Sahametrei also of Cambodia in 2008. He joined the MHOSLJ and in 1999 was appointed Grand Prior of the New Zealand jurisdiction, a post he has retained to date with a brief interlude during 2009-2011 [GM Decree 16/09]. In 2009, he was appointed a member of the International Grand Magistral Council serving also as Deputy Grand Hospitaller, subsequently serving on the Grand Executive Council. In 2015, he was appointed Grand Hospitaller of the Order, a post he retained until 2020. He currently serves as Grand Hospitaller Emeritus.[31]

---

[31] Professor Brett Delahunt. Wellington School of Medicine and Health Sciences, University of Otago,

Prof. Charles Savona-Ventura GCLJ KMLJ SCLJ (1955---) received his M.D. from the University of Malta (1979) and his D.Sc.Med. from the Institute of Mother and Child in Warsaw (1999). In the interim, he underwent specialist training in the field of obstetrics and gynaecology and medical obstetrics obtaining fellowships to the Royal College of Obstetrician & Gynaecologist (UK), and the Royal Colleges of Physicians of Ireland and of Edinburgh. He currently serves on the Examination and Quality Assurance Committees of European Board and College of Obstetrics and Gynaecology (EBCOG). During his career, he contributed to the delivery of specialist care in the speciality within the national Maltese Health Service and to medical education at the University of Malta. He currently serves as Professor and Head of Department of Obstetrics & Gynaecology and Director for the University Centre for Traditional Chinese Medicine. He also teaches medical history and sociology within the Institute for Baroque Studies and the Faculty of Social Sciences. He joined the MHOSLJ in 2004 [GC No. 6751] and served the Maltese jurisdiction in the role of historian, hospitaller, and eventually Grand Prior serving also as honorary president of the jurisdiction's two registered voluntary organization. On the international front, he has served the Order in the office of Grand Archivist & Historian (2013-2022) and subsequently as Grand Hospitaller (2021 et sec). He also serves as the director of the registered voluntary academic organization, *Academia Internationalis Sancti Lazari Ordinis*, which aims to promote and disseminate research related to the history of the Order and other chivalric organizations. His interest in medical history led to the publication about the history of the Order of Saint Lazarus: *The Hospitaller Knights of Saint Lazarus* [published by the Grand Priory of the Maltese Islands, MHOSLJ, 2019, +605p., illustrated ISBN 978-99957-1-439-0][32]

Annual Hospitaller Reports

From conception, the primary onus of the Office of the Grand Hospitaller was to coordinate the charitable works of the International Order. The first attempt to present a report from the office of the Grand Hospitaller was made during the Grand Magistral Council held in Liege on the 3-4th June 1972. The report, incorporated within that of the Grand Chancellor, simply stated:

WORKS CARRIED OUT DURING THE PAST YEAR –
The following are some of the charitable works carried out during the past year: The Commandery of Lochore ran an Ambulance Service in Scotland; an Emergency Ambulance Service was run in New Zealand,

---

[32] Available from https://www.lulu.com/en/gb/shop/charles-savona-ventura/the-hospitaller-knights-of-saint-lazarus/hardcover/product-1g26ppw2.html

where also medicinal drugs and other commodities were supplied to Leprosaria. A large quantity of pharmaceutical drugs, to the approximate value of US$20,000, which were provided by the Grand Priory of the U.S.A., was shipped from Malta to the St. Joseph Leprosarium in Abony-Davougon, Dahomey. In Victoria, Australia, a Clinic run by Chev. Dr. von Moger was placed under the aegis of the Order. This is an incomplete report of the activities of the Order as only a few jurisdictions have submitted a report on the activities carried out by them. [33]

No further conglomerated philanthropic reports were apparently presented in the subsequent Grand Magistral Council meetings, though jurisdictional reports of philanthropic activities carried out in the outgoing years were individually presented by the Heads of Jurisdictions in the various Grand Magistral Council meetings held in Malta (1973)[34], Malta (1977)[35], and Edinburgh (1980)[36].

---

[33] MHOSLJ. Report of the Grand Magistral Council held in Liege, 3rd and 4th June 1972 - Continuation of List of Members, Amendments, and Audited Account. MHOSLJ, Malta, 1972, +24pp.

[34] MHOSLJ. The Military and Hospitaller Order of Saint Lazarus of Jerusalem - Inauguration of the Grand Chancery, Malta; Report of the Chapter General held on 11th and 12th May 1973 - Continuation of list of members, amendments to list of members. MHOSLJ, 1973, +14pp.

[35] MHOSLJ. Report of the Grand Magistral Council held in Malta 23rd - 24th September 1977. MHOSLJ, Malta, 1977, +20pp.

[36] MHOSLJ. The Military and Hospitaller Order of Saint Lazarus of Jerusalem - Report of the Grand Magistral Council held in Edinburgh, Scotland, 23rd-24th June 1980. MHOSLJ, 1980, +48pp.

During the Grand Magistral Council meeting held in Helsinki on the 7-8th September 1982, a dedicated report from the Grand Hospitallers was presented in addition to the individual jurisdictional reports.[37] In that report, it was noted that, in December 1980, queries from the media about the worldwide charitable activities of the Order could not be properly responded to. Thus, the Office of the Grand Hospitaller undertook a questionnaire study to elicit details about the hospitaller activities of the Order as a whole and to determine whether there was any interest among the twenty-seven extant jurisdictions regarding a major joint project *which would bring worldwide recognition to the Order of Saint Lazarus.* Fourteen jurisdictions responded giving a list of their charitable activities during the period 1980-81 with a monetary contribution amounting to a total of US$2,233,800. The response also indicated that the jurisdictions preferred to confine their charitable programs to their own pet projects. However, a number of potential Grand Hospitaller projects were proposed:

a) Setting up an annually or biennial award in the field of medicine given to an individual who has made a significant scientific contribution under difficult circumstances.

b) Supporting the setting up of a hospital in Malta under the name of Saint Lazarus of Jerusalem administered by the Maltese government and regular local staff supplemented by volunteer physicians from the Order.

---

[37] MHOSLJ. The Military and Hospitaller Order of Saint Lazarus of Jerusalem - Report of the Magistral Council held in Helsinki, Finland 7th-8th September 1982. MHOSLJ, 1982, +74pp.

c) Setting up a program of support for Christians in the Holy Land.

In addition, the Grand Bailiwick of Germany proposed the formation of a permanent commission of the national organisations of charity of the Order and its branches to discuss the international actions relating to charity.[38]

The initiative to present a global Grand Hospitaller Report was apparently not maintained and the subsequent Grand Magistral Council meetings held in Washington (1984)[39], Salzburg (1990)[40] and Spain (1992)[41] saw again the presentation of individual jurisdictional reports rather than a global one. In 1994, an attempt was made to list the humanitarian work being carried out by different jurisdictions of the Order. This however appears simply to be a list of activities reported by the different jurisdictions rather than an attempt at providing a comprehensive international report.[42]

---

[38] MHOSLJ, 1982, pp.58-67.

[39] MHOSLJ. The Military and Hospitaller Order of Saint Lazarus of Jerusalem - Report of the Magistral Council held in Washington, D.C., USA 12th to 15th July 1984. MHOSLJ, 1984, +84pp.

[40] MHOSLJ. The Military and Hospitaller Order of St. Lazarus of Jerusalem - Report of the Grand Magistral Council held in Salzburg 26th to 29th October 1990. MHOSLJ, 1990, +32pp.

[41] MHOSLJ. The Military and Hospitaller Order of Saint Lazarus of Jerusalem - Report of the Grand Magistral Council Castle of Albatarrec, Lerida, Spain 14th to 18th May 1992. MHOSLJ, 1992, +70pp.

[42] Humanitarian work being carried out by different jurisdictions of our Order. Saint Lazarus Newsletter, May 1994, 2:pp.2-4; September 1994, 3:pp.2-4.

HUMANITARIAN WORK BEING CARRIED OUT BY DIFFERENT JURISDIC-
TIONS OF OUR ORDER.

1. Inauguration of the Saint Lazarus Chapel in the Hospital of Salgotarjan, Hungary, entirely refurbished by
   the Order.

2. Assistance of various kinds to physically handicapped
   people in Turkey, USA, Portugal, Marocco, Spain and
   Cyprus.

3. Participation by members of our Order in the United
   Nation Austria Field Hospital Itan (UNAFHIR) to help
   refugees from Iraq.

4. Charitable aid for Croatia.

5. Participation of a number of our members in the visit
   of H.H. Pope Johannes Paul II in Hungary and organising

   transportation of physically handicapped people in
   Mariopoes and in Budapest.

6. Establishment of a Saint Lazarus foundation in England for sick children.

7. In Helsinki, Finland, the Order has several drug am-
   bulances and one special rescue unit. Members of the
   Order work with epileptics. The Order provides catastrophe phones for elderly and disabled people
   living alone.

8. Swedish support for a secondary school student in
   Haiti.

9. Swedish provision of medicin to poor sick people in
   Bobo-Dioulasso in Burkina Faso.

10. In Malta assistance and provision of equipment to an
    "Old Persons Home" run by the Little sisters of the
    poor and to Saint Joseph orphanage for children.

11. In Malte the Leprosorium is supported by the Order.

12. The Order supports institutions for handicapped in
    Malte such as Id-Dar Tal-Providenza and Friendship
    Park as well as the Youth Institution St. Francis
    Ravelin.

13. In Cologne in Germany the local organization of the
    German Multiple Schlerosis Society is being entirely
    supported financially by our members.

14. In Germany a new foundation with an initial capital of DEM 300.000 has been set up for the care of the orphaned and the single handicapped people.

15. In Frechen in Germany more than a hundred handicapped and old people live in the Gold Kraemer House in appartments which were built for their special needs. These people are also entirely supported and looked after 24 hours a day.

16. In Pulheim in Germany more than 120 handicapped persons are being taken care of in a house provided by the Order.

17. In the territory of the commandery of Berlin-Branden burg in Germany an amount of DEM 75.000 is paid in assistance to the needy.

18. From Germany medicines and various medical equipmen have been sent to Russia, Hungary and Croatia to the amount of DEM 2.300.000.

19. From Germany medicines are supplied to the lepers in the Republic of Benin to the amount of DEM 1.000.00(

20. The German assistance to Czechoslovakia amounts to DEM 612.000.

21. From Alsace medicines are supplied to lepers in Cameroon, and several lepers are looked after by members of the Order.

22. In Auckland in New Zealand the Leprosy Research Unit of the School of Medicine is sponsered by the Order, as is the Leprosy Trust Board, now known as the Pacific Leprosy Foundation.

23. In the USA financial contributions are made by the Order to the American Leprosy Mission.

24. From Malte material and financial assistance as well as missionaries are sent to leper colonies in Egypt.

25. The St. Lazarus Foundation is recognized by WHO specificially for Aids but is also a member of the ILEF (the International Leprosy Association).

This list of humanitarian work being carried out by different jurisdictions of the Order is not complete.

However, in the subsequent years, no attempt appears to have been made to consolidate and report comprehensively on the humanitarian work being performed by the various jurisdictions of the Order though the various jurisdictions were encouraged to present their biennial philanthropic reports during the Grand Magistral Council meeting.[43] The 1999-2000 review of hospitaller work of twelve jurisdictions were published in the first issue of the International Report of the then Paris Obedience *The Green Cross – La Croix de Sinople*. The reporting jurisdictions included America, Australia, Austria, Brazil, Canada, Czech Republic, England & Wales, France, Germany and LHW, Sweden, Switzerland, and Zimbabwe.[44]

This status quo remained the same well until 2004. The incumbent Grand Hospitaller at the time reported that: *in recent memory, although individual jurisdictions of the Order report on their finances to the Grand Chancery on an annual basis, there has not been a consolidated report or assessment of charitable activities of the Order on a global basis.* A move was made in May 2002 to solicit philanthropy information from the various jurisdiction, however only 16 out of the 39 jurisdictions provided a report.[45]

---

[43] Saint Lazarus Newsletter, December 1997, 11:p.2.

[44] Bennet-England, Rodney [editor]. The Green Cross – La Croix de Sinople: 1999/2000 International Report. 2020, 1:p.12-38 [available https://mhoslj.weebly.com/uploads/4/8/0/0/48006361/1999-2000_bulletin_international.pdf]

[45] Moritsugu, Kenneth. Report to the Grand Magistral Council of 2001-2002. Report of the Grand Magistral Council Meeting 2003 held in Vaals, Netherlands 8-11th May 2003, +1p.

The subsequent years were characterised by a period of turmoil, strife, and reorganization for the Order. This appears to have rather placed the solicitation of philanthropic reports on the backburner, though different jurisdictions continued with their charitable activities.

In 2011, the first of a series of annual Grand Hospitaller reports were issued starting with the outgoing year 2010. The Grand Prior of the Order Chev. Dr. Ronald H.M. Hendriks wrote: *As far as I know this is the first time we can give you an overview (unfortunately not complete yet) about the hospitaller activities of the Order.* That year a total of €3,995,371 and an unspecified number of volunteer man-hours were donated supporting a wide variety of charitable activities.[46]

There has since been a regular annual review of the philanthropic work being performed globally by the international Order.

- Moritsugu, Kenneth. Military and Hospitaller Order of Saint Lazarus of Jerusalem - 2010 Annual Report. MHOSLJ, 2011, +22p.

- Mittelstaedt, Axel. The Military and Hospitaller Order of St. Lazarus of Jerusalem. International 2011 Hospitaller Report. MHOSLJ, 2012

- Mittelstaedt, Axel. The Military and Hospitaller Order of St. Lazarus of Jerusalem. International 2012 Hospitaller Report. MHOSLJ, 2013

- Mittelstaedt, Axel. The Military and Hospitaller Order of St. Lazarus of Jerusalem. International 2013 Hospitaller Report. MHOSLJ, 2014

---

[46] MHOSLJ. Military and Hospitaller Order of Saint Lazarus of Jerusalem - 2010 Annual Report. MHOSLJ, 2011, +22p.

- Mittelstaedt, Axel. The Military and Hospitaller Order of St. Lazarus of Jerusalem. International 2014 Hospitaller Report. MHOSLJ, 2015
- Delahunt, Brett. The Military and Hospitaller Order of St. Lazarus of Jerusalem. International 2015 Hospitaller Report. MHOSLJ, 2016
- Delahunt, Brett. The Military and Hospitaller Order of St. Lazarus of Jerusalem. International 2016 Hospitaller Report. MHOSLJ, 2017
- Delahunt, Brett. The Military and Hospitaller Order of St. Lazarus of Jerusalem. International 2017 Hospitaller Report. MHOSLJ, 2018
- Delahunt, Brett. The Military and Hospitaller Order of St. Lazarus of Jerusalem. International 2018 Hospitaller Report. MHOSLJ, 2019
- Savona-Ventura, Charles. The Military and Hospitaller Order of St. Lazarus of Jerusalem. International 2019 Hospitaller Report. MHOSLJ, 2020
- Savona-Ventura, Charles. The Military and Hospitaller Order of St. Lazarus of Jerusalem. International 2020 Hospitaller Report. MHOSLJ, 2021

An attempt was made to formalize the structure of the individual reports submitted by the hospitallers representing the various jurisdictions to ensure that a suitable description of the charity being supported was provided. In addition, appreciation was given to volunteer man-hours dedicated to philanthropy. This is difficult to truly quantify and translate into monetary value, however each volunteer man-hour was given an arbitrary value of €10.[47] The Byelaws of the Order require the heads of jurisdictions to forward the report for the outgoing year by the 31st March.

---

[47] Delahunt, Brett. Guideline for drawing up the Hospitaller Report. MHOSLJ, 2019, +1p.; Savona-Ventura, Charles. Jurisdictional Hospitaller Report form. MHOSLJ, 2020, +7pp.

Byelaw Art. 3.12   *ANNUAL REPORTS OF HOSPITALLER, CHARITABLE AND OTHER WORKS*

Each Jurisdiction is required to submit an annual report to the Vice-Grand Chancellor (administration) not later than the 31st March of the following year, detailing all hospitaller and charitable activities within the jurisdiction. The annual Hospitaller report shall also be sent to the grand Hospitaller by the same date. [48]

---

[48] MHOSLJ. The By-Laws of the Order. Agreed by the GMC, 3 November 2018, p.11.

Charitable Activities of the Order - overview

The reports published during the decade 2010-2019 have highlighted the overall philanthropic contributions that have been made annually by the various jurisdictions in recent years. Unfortunately, the reports, especially the earlier ones, are not complete since some jurisdictions failed to return a report and details provided may not be equitable to later reports. The non-equity of the reports and the broad classifications used from year-to-year makes it difficult to fully and accurately compare the annual distribution of the donations reported. In addition, the earlier reports did not factor in the volunteer man-hours that were eventually valued at €10 per hour. However, the reports do indicate preferential trends that reflect the needs of the developed and developing world communities.

The health needs in the modern world depend on the socio-economic status of any particular community, region, or country, and thus the health need priorities of communities in the developed countries are very different from those living in developing countries. In the latter, the health need requirements are primarily related to ensuring the provision of adequate nutrition, safe water resources, and means to combat infections. These interventions would further mitigate the high childhood mortality prevalent in these communities.

In developed countries, the health support priorities are very different. In these, the main causes of ill-health and mortality are chronic non-communicable conditions brought about by the consequences of modern lifestyle, which promote metabolic and cardiovascular disease. The needs in developed communities, especially highly developed ones, are generally related to hospice care of invalid persons with problems of chronic illness and of advancing age.

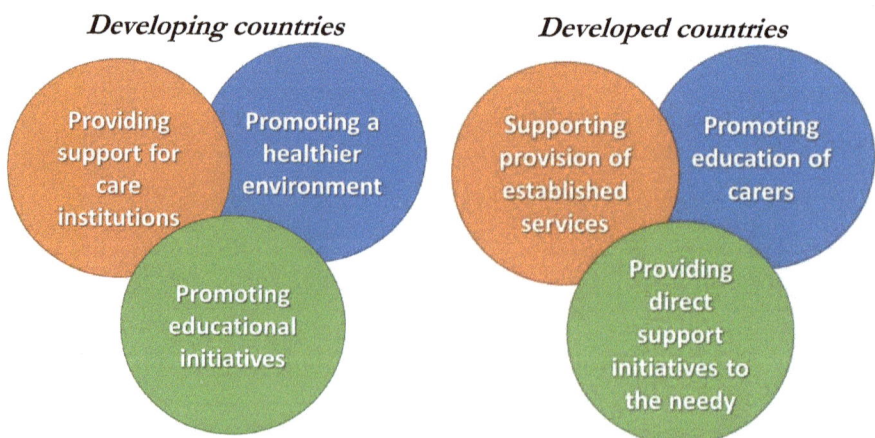

Philanthropic pillars essential to support the needy

Throughout the decade 2010-2019, a total of €25,144,951[49] were donated by the various jurisdictions. This figure excludes the donation made by the voluntary organizations associated to the Humanitarian Grand

---

[49] The figure includes the donations made by the Grand Priory of the Maltese Islands for the year 2010 – the report had not been incorporated withing the overall International Report. Total amount donated: €25,749.

Priory Europe – notably the Lazarus relief organizations in Poland [LAZARUS Ermland-Maßuren] and in Germany [LAZARUS Hilfswerk (LHW)] who contribute significantly accounting for 82.7% of the total donations. In 2020, whereas the national and hereditary jurisdictions contributed a total of €2,614,746 in monetary, in-kind, and volunteer man-hour donations, the V/Os of the Humanitarian Grand Priory Europe contributed a further €11,590,581. The contribution made by these V/O organizations will be reviewed separately from the donations made by the national and hereditary jurisdictions.

Year	National & Hereditary jurisdictions	V/O Humanitarian Grand Priory Europe
2010	€4,001,891	Not stated
2011	€2,300,000	Not stated
2012	€3,964,600	Not stated
2013	€2,609,810	Not stated
2014	€2,883,151	€8,000,000
2015	€1,532,583	€8,400,000
2016	€1,969,646	€9,318,941
2017	€1,724,130	€9,628,050
2018	€2,066,551	€10,743,790
2019	€2,092,589	€12,403,235
2020	€2,614,746	€11,590,581

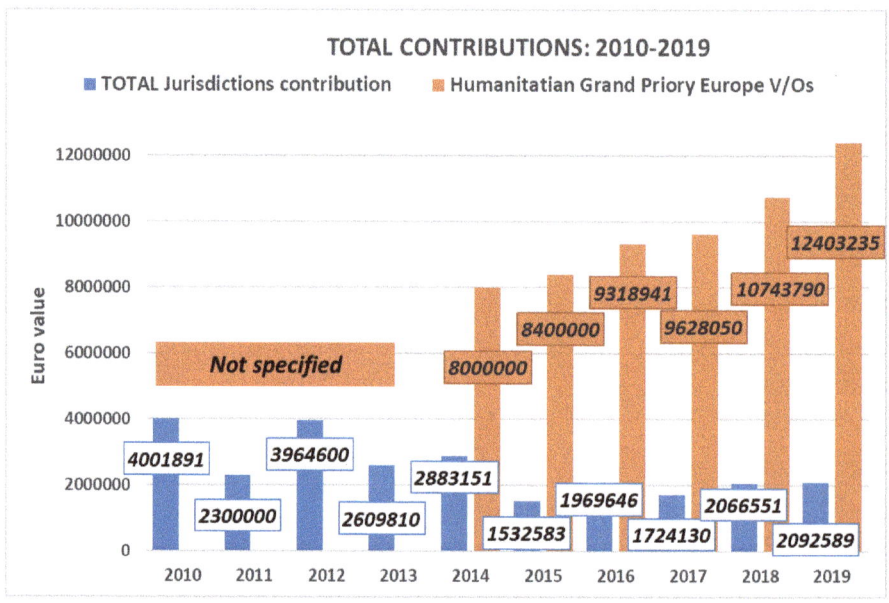

Hansen's Disease - Leprosy

Since its origins outside the walls of Jerusalem, the brethren of the Order of Saint Lazarus have been concerned primarily with the care of victims of the dreaded disease leprosy. This *raison d'être* has been retained down to modern times. The Constitution [50] clearly defines the aims of the modern-day Order as:

> *ARTICLE 3.1 AIMS OF THE ORDER*
>
> *The aims of the Order are: .... To assist, succour and help the poor, the sick and the afflicted, especially those suffering from leprosy or similar diseases without distinction of religion, race, origin or age.*

---

[50] MHOSLJ. The Constitution of the Military and Hospitaller Order of Saint Lazarus of Jerusalem. Agreed by the Joint Reunification Commission, Toronto 18 February 2006/Amended 11 March 2006, revised 21 September 2015, p.1.

Leprosy (now referred to as Hansen's Disease to disassociate the infection from past stigma of the disease) is caused by an infection with the bacterium *Mycobacterium leprae*. Like the bacterium causing Tuberculosis, these bacteria grow very slowly but steadily cause disability from damage to the nerves resulting in the affected areas losing the ability to sense touch and pain. This will lead to repeated injuries, like cuts and burns, exposing the individual to chronic secondary infections, including osteomyelitis causing the affected digits to be destroyed and reabsorb, resulting in the apparent loss of toes and fingers. The nerve damage can also result in paralysis of hands and feet. Corneal ulcers and blindness can also occur if facial nerves are affected. The affected nerves can also swell up causing nodular growth. Other stigmata of the disease include skin changes that are represented by lighter or darker patches, often dry or flaky, with loss of feeling, or reddish due to inflammation of the skin. With advanced disease, there may also be loss of eyebrows and saddle-nose deformity resulting from damage to the nasal septum. Fortunately, in today's world, effective treatment with multiple antibiotic therapy [Multi-Drug Therapy – MDT] is available. Early diagnosis and treatment can therefore generally prevent disability that can result from the disease, and people with Hansen's disease can continue to work and lead an active life.

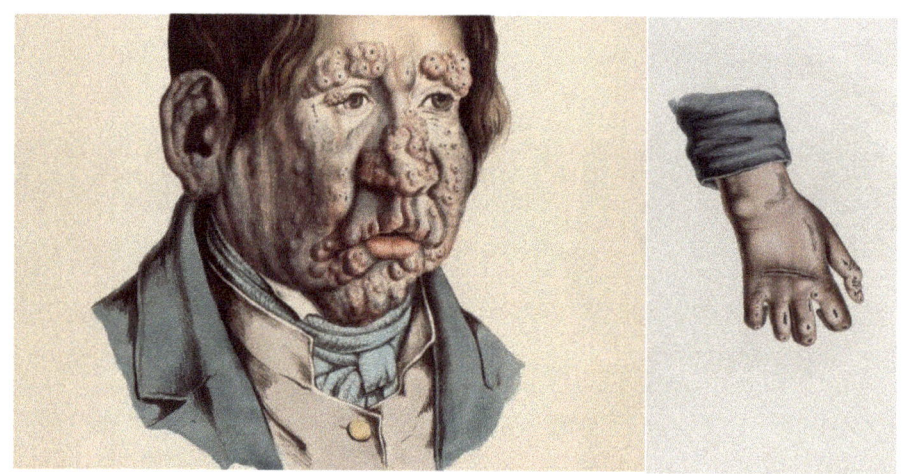

The pharmaceutical company Novartis® which produces these medications has, since 2000, donated more than 68 million blister packs of MDT through the W.H.O., helping to treat more than 7.3 million patients worldwide. A new agreement extended the program to 2025. In the words of the Chief Operating Officer for Global Health at Novartis Dr Lutz Hegemann: *"Leprosy can be cured and prevented. With a comprehensive approach, we can see the end of leprosy. By supplying this treatment free of charge to WHO over the last 20 years we have helped over seven million people be cured of leprosy. We look forward to helping increasingly few over the coming years."*

The free availability of this effective treatment has led to an overall decrease in global prevalence, but not to the total annihilation of the disease. The drop in global incidence is not equitable throughout the world. Developing countries still see significant numbers of new cases being diagnosed annually. The large majority of new cases are reported from

Southeast Asia. In addition, many prior victims of Hansen's Disease remain marginalized and handicapped because of the chronic complications of the infection.

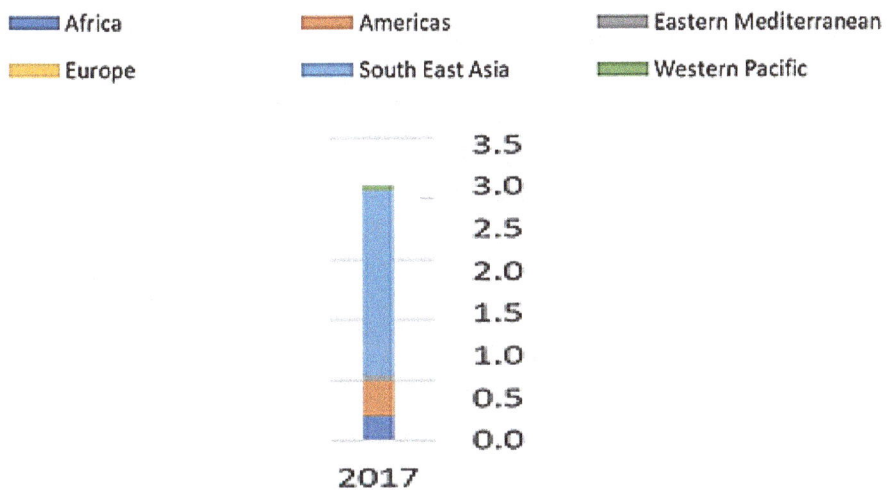

Global incidence [newly diagnosed cases per 100 000 population] in 2017

[51]

In its Global Leprosy Strategy 2021–2030, the W.H.O. has proposed an action program aiming towards achieving Zero Leprosy.[52] The program is structured around 4 core pillars:

- Pillar I: Implement integrated country-owned zero leprosy roadmaps in all endemic countries.

[51] After W.H.O. Epidemiology - Leprosy Epidemiological situation 2017, burden and distribution. W.H.O., Geneva, 2018, http://origin.searo.who.int/entity/global_leprosy_programme/epidemiology/en/
[52] W.H.O. Towards zero leprosy – Global Leprosy (Hansen's Disease) Strategy 2021-2030. W.H.O., Geneva, 2021, +30pp.

- Pillar II: Scale up leprosy prevention alongside integrated active case detection.
- Pillar III: Manage leprosy and its complications and prevent new disability.
- Pillar IV: Combat stigma and ensure human rights are respected.

It would be well for the jurisdictional hospitallers of the Order to read through the W.H.O. report [53] to ensure that funds supporting Leprosy Campaigns are directed to projects having maximum efficacy in the light of the W.H.O. program. As an Order, we should also work towards raising awareness about leprosy and inform people about its curability thus striving to remove the stigma associated with the condition. We should involve ourselves wholeheartedly to celebrate World Leprosy Day, observed on the last Sunday of January each year, established in 1954 by French philanthropist Raoul Follereau.

WORLD LEPROSY DAY
Last Sunday of January

In the decade under review, a reported total of €2,942,556 have been donated by various jurisdictions to support the fight against the ravages of Hansen's Disease and thus alleviate the suffering of its victims. This sum comprises about 13.5% of the total philanthropic donations made by the

---

[53] Downloaded from https://www.who.int/publications/i/item/9789290228509

jurisdictions.[54] In 2020, the amount donated to support the fight against Hansen's Disease amounted to a total of €386,595 [14.8% of the total amount donated by the jurisdictions].

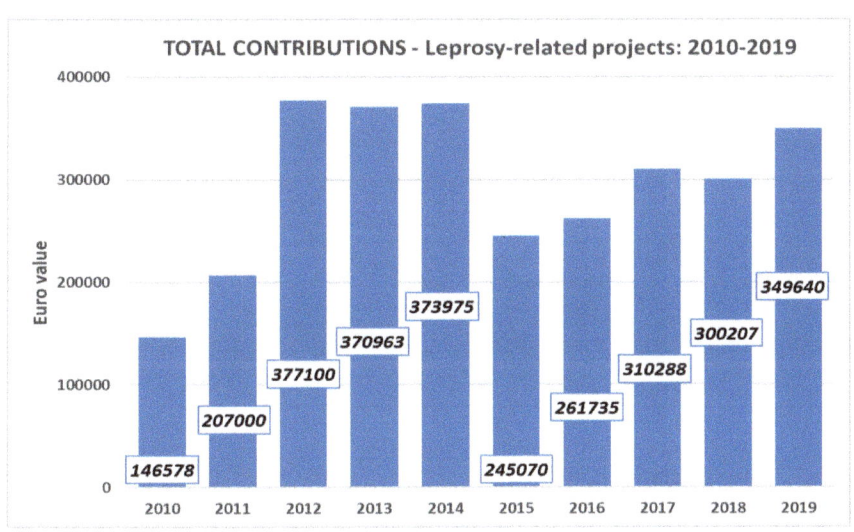

Palliative & Care of the Aged – Healthcare support

Healthcare support priorities in the developed world are very different from those in developing countries. The main causes of ill-health and mortality are chronic non-communicable conditions brought about by the consequences of modern lifestyle, which promote metabolic and cardiovascular disease. The needs in developed communities, especially highly developed ones, are generally related to hospice care of invalid

---

[54] The 2010 data from the Grand Priory of the Maltese Islands was not included in the Grand Hospitaller's report for the year. The relevant donation of €17,303 has been added to the overall total.

persons with problems of chronic illness, and problems of advancing age. Individuals in long-term care face health and social problems that may not be effectively and completely covered by the formal support systems in place in that community. Problems related to the care of the invalid elderly in both the developed and developing world have increased exponentially over the last six decades, though there still remains a significant divide between the two.

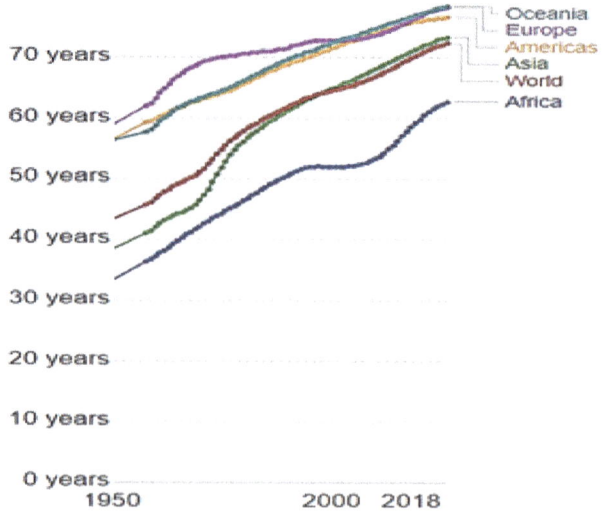

Trends in Life expectancy by region

In reviewing the country-by-country distribution of the philanthropic activities of the Order, it is clear that the majority of resources target the developed world in general and particularly the exigencies which result from ill-health or old age. This is in line with the general healthcare and social needs of the developed world. There is increasing scope to continue supporting this philanthropic category without, of course, neglecting other areas of need [e.g., childcare and family support, persons with special needs, etc.]. The support given to Palliative/Aged Care & Medical Support by the national jurisdictions varies considerably, ranging from providing support to institutions to help improve their services and maintain their day-to-day management, to providing educational training for carers, and direct support to inmates. These three facets of support are important and must be maintained. The provision of support to ensure better services for the needy is an important indirect means of improving individuals' wellbeing. The National jurisdictions are, however, encouraged to seek and explore a more direct approach to ameliorate the lives of these individuals. Such direct approaches can assume many different formats – regular social personal visits, providing entertainment opportunities, etc. These direct approach initiatives may not appear as grand on paper as do indirect support initiatives, but the former do have a major role to play in ensuring the mental wellbeing of dependants in care.

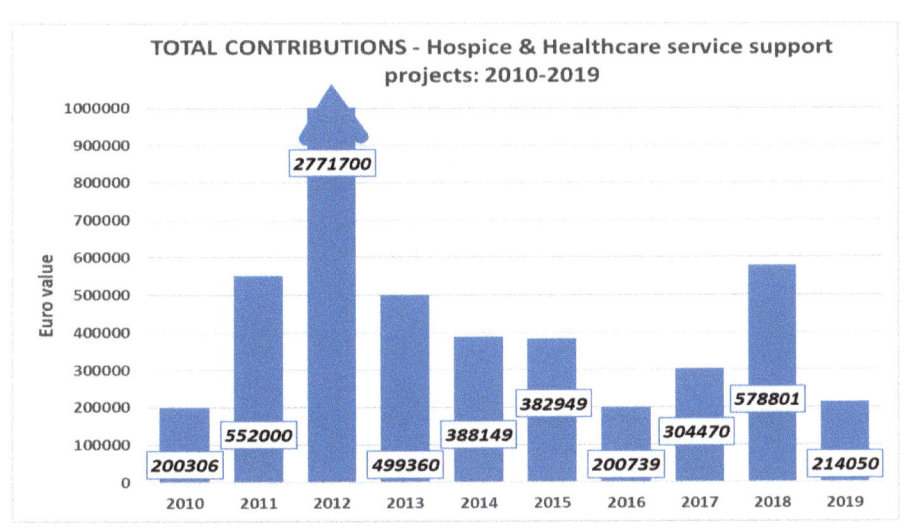

In the decade under review, a reported total of €6,092,524 have been donated by various jurisdictions to support the fight against the problems related to palliative care, care of the elderly, and healthcare services support. This sum comprises about 28.0% of the total philanthropic donations made by the jurisdictions.[55] In 2020, the amount donated to support palliative care and care of the elderly amounted to a total of €250,518 [9.6% of the total amount donated by the jurisdictions].

In addition, the contributions made by the voluntary organizations associated to the Humanitarian Grand Priory Europe – the Lazarus relief organizations in Poland [LAZARUS Ermland-Maßuren] and in Germany [LAZARUS Hilfswerk (LHW)] – mainly target palliative care, care of the elderly and general medical support. Throughout the period 2014-2019, the voluntary organizations donated a total of €58,494,016 [*data for 2010-2013 unavailable*]. In 2020, these organizations contributed a total of €11,590,581 in monetary, in-kind, and volunteer man-hour donations.

---

[55] The 2010 data from the Grand Priory of the Maltese Islands was not included in the Grand Hospitaller's report for the year. The relevant donation of €650 has been added to the overall total.

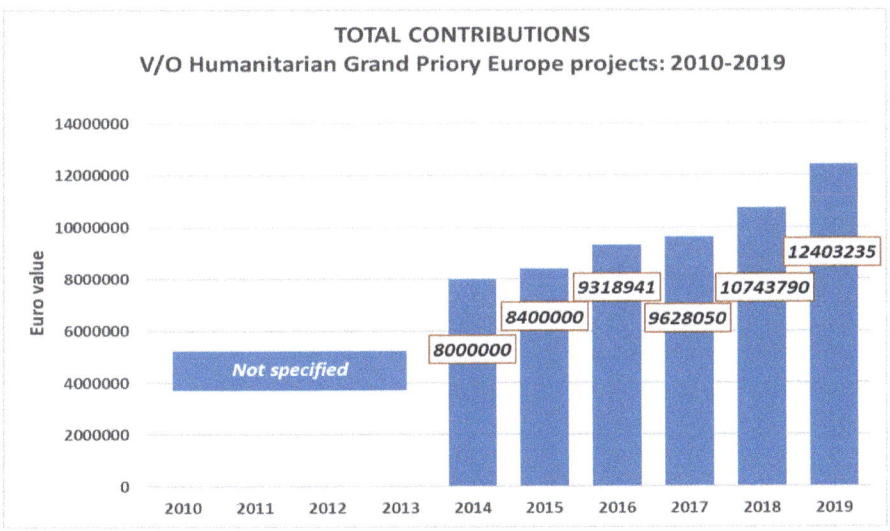

TOTAL CONTRIBUTIONS
V/O Humanitarian Grand Priory Europe projects: 2010-2019

Further support was given to individuals with special needs. In the decade under review, a reported total of €530,390 have been donated by various jurisdictions to support the fight against the problems related to palliative care, care of the elderly, and healthcare services support. This sum comprises about 2.4% of the total philanthropic donations made by the jurisdictions.[56] In 2020, the amount donated to support palliative care and care of the elderly amounted to a total of €81,223 [3.1% of the total amount donated by the jurisdictions].

---

[56] The 2010 data from the Grand Priory of the Maltese Islands was not included in the Grand Hospitaller's report for the year. The relevant donation of €2796 has been added to the overall total.

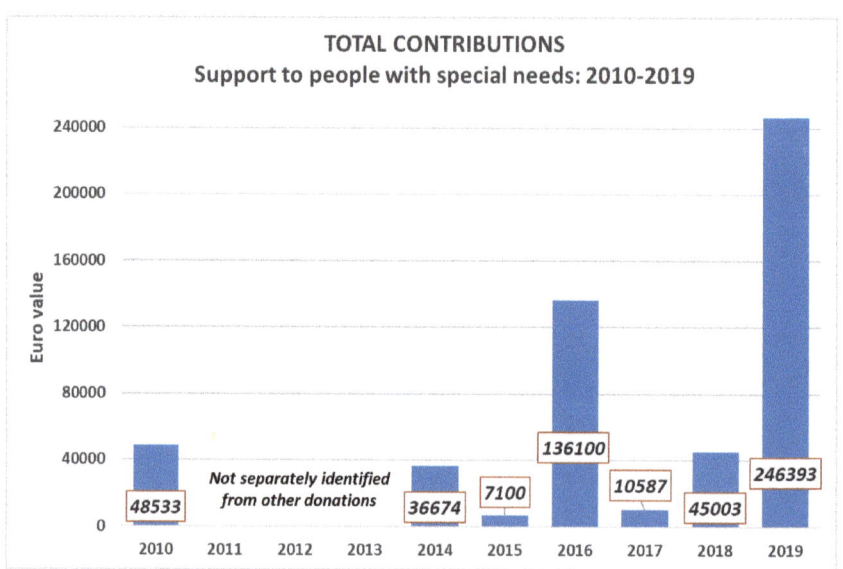

TOTAL CONTRIBUTIONS
Support to people with special needs: 2010-2019

Child & Family Services support

A particular area of concern in the developing world is childhood mortality generally brought about by malnutrition and gastrointestinal infections caused mainly by compromised water supplies. Childhood mortality rates in Africa and Asia amount to up to 20% of total births. In contrast, Europe, North America, and Australia report a childhood mortality of <1% [see Figure below]. However, even in the developed world, children from disadvantaged families remain at risk for future discrimination and social disadvantages in the society they live in. Support for these young needy in society is essential, not only to reduce their immediate suffering, but also to provide them with the necessary educational background to make them valuable survivors in the competitive world they live in.

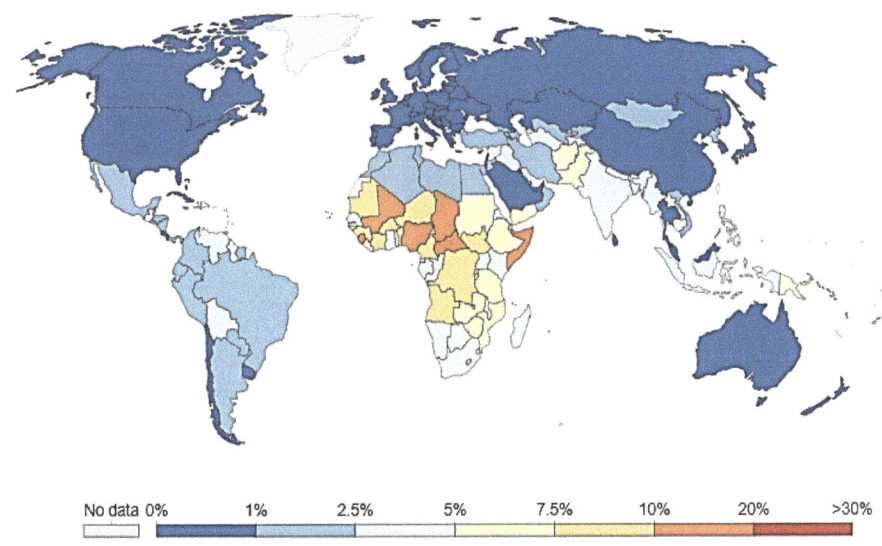

| No data | 0% | 1% | 2.5% | 5% | 7.5% | 10% | 20% | >30% |

Childhood mortality rate, 2017 – Deaths under 5 years of age [57]

In the decade under review, a reported total of €2,395,393 have been donated by various jurisdictions to support the fight against the problems related to childcare and family support projects. This sum comprises about 11.0% of the total philanthropic donations made by the jurisdictions.[58] In 2020, the amount donated to support childcare and family support projects amounted to a total of €402,268 [15.4% of the total amount donated by the jurisdictions].

---

[57] UN Inter-agency Group for Child Mortality Estimation. OurWorldInData.org/child-mortality

[58] The 2010 data from the Grand Priory of the Maltese Islands was not included in the Grand Hospitaller's report for the year. The relevant donation of €3500 has been added to the overall total.

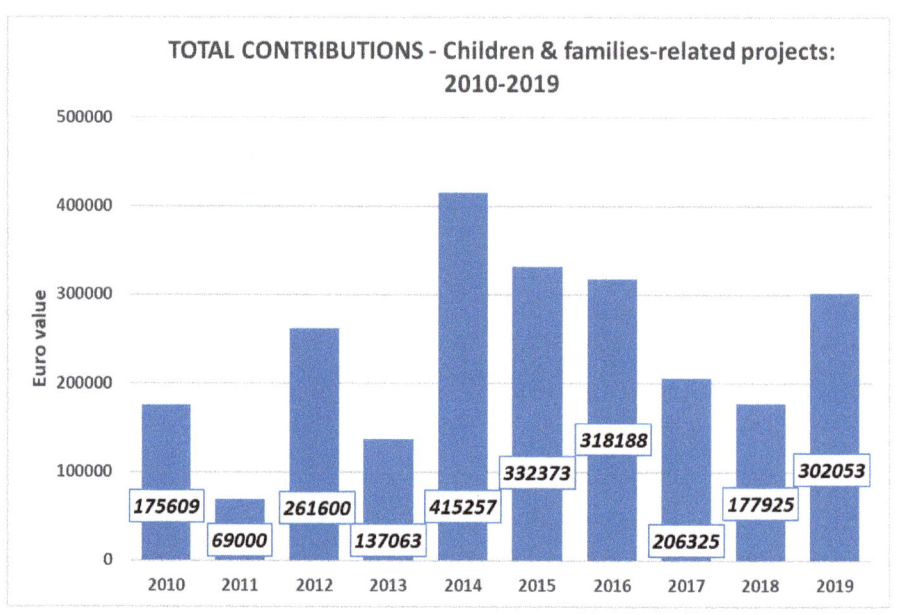

TOTAL CONTRIBUTIONS - Children & families-related projects: 2010-2019

Values shown: 175609, 69000, 261600, 137063, 415257, 332373, 318188, 206325, 177925, 302053

Community Services, food campaigns & support for the homeless

The various jurisdictions have undertaken support projects to help individuals or groups in the community by providing community services, organizing food distribution campaigns, and providing support for the needy and homeless. In the decade under review, a reported total of €2,412,991 have been donated by various jurisdictions to support food campaign projects and support for the homeless. This sum comprises about 11.1% of the total philanthropic donations made by the jurisdictions. In addition, a further €2,936,177 [13.5% of total] were directed towards the support community service provision. In 2020, the respective figures were €394,432 [15.1%] and €287335 [11.0%].

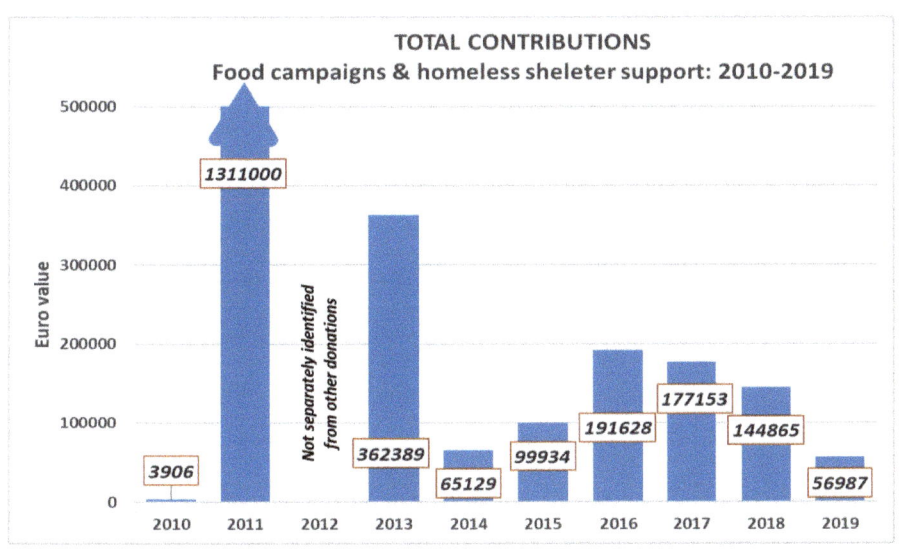

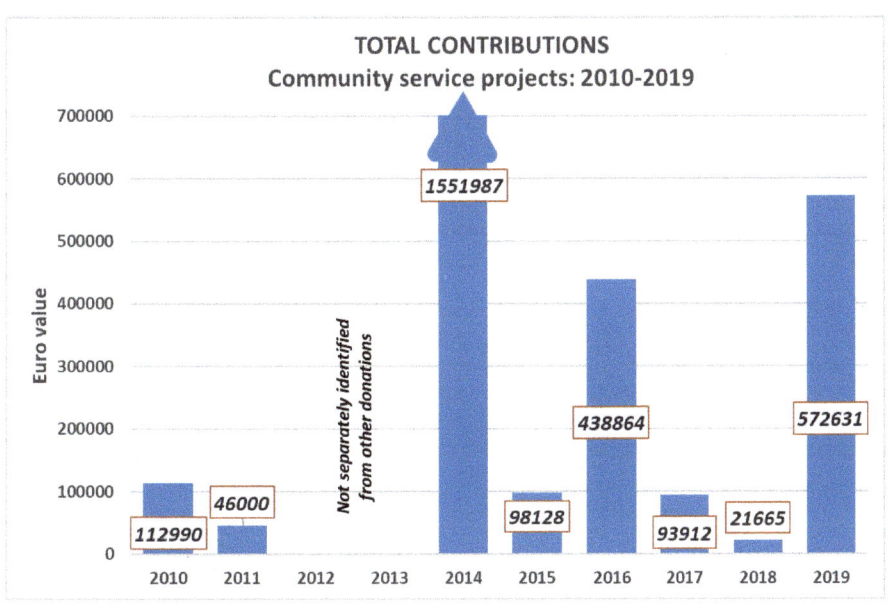

International & missionary projects support and emergency support measures

The various jurisdictions have undertaken support for international and missionary-based projects generally in the developing countries to help groups in the community. Support was also given to communities in need following a major natural or man-made disaster. In the decade under review, a reported total of €5,248,359 [24.1% of the total] have been donated by various jurisdictions to support international and missionary projects; while a further sum of €425,948 [2.0% of the total] was made available for emergency support measures.[59] In 2020, the respective figures were €572,057 [21.9%] and €96,649 [3.7%].

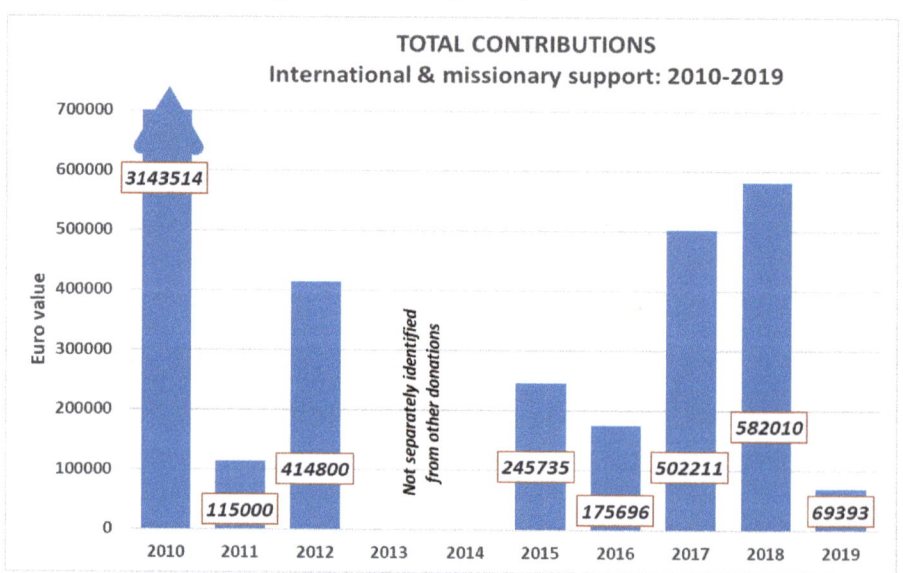

[59] The 2010 data from the Grand Priory of the Maltese Islands was not included in the Grand Hospitaller's report for the year. The relevant donation of €1000 and €500 respectively has been added to the overall total.

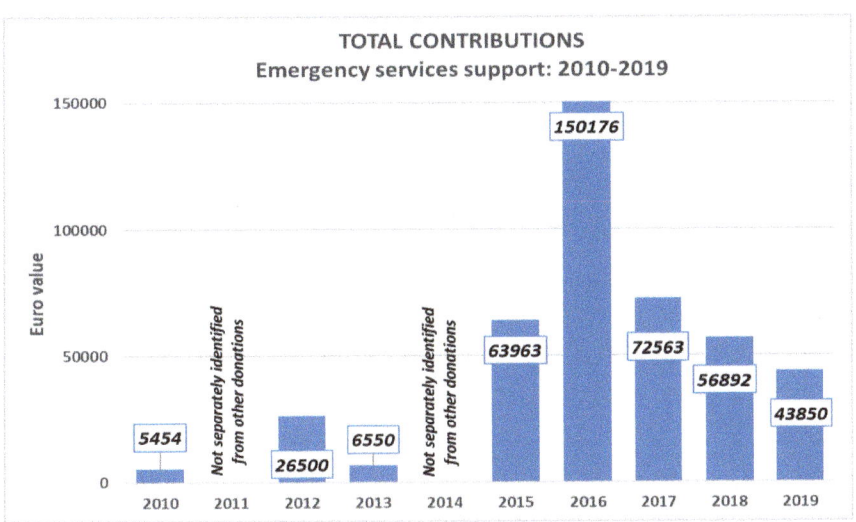

TOTAL CONTRIBUTIONS
Emergency services support: 2010-2019

A further number of donations have been classified as a miscellaneous group. Over the decade in review, these account for a total of €2,145,613 [9.9% of the total]. In 2020, the amount reported was €133,219 [5.1%].

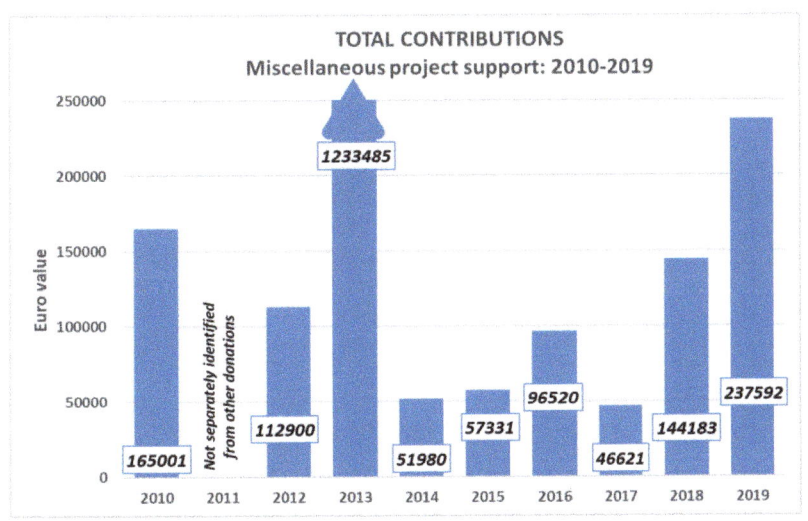

TOTAL CONTRIBUTIONS
Miscellaneous project support: 2010-2019

It is clear that a definite classification of philanthropic activities needs to be developed to ensure that more accurate annual comparisons can be made in the future. The following classification may serve to paint a more accurate equitable picture of the actual charitable activities of the Order on an international level. It is important that the submitted report would also include details about each charity and which continent/country it targeted.

Charitable activity	Definition
• Leprosy-related programs	This category should include any project that targets the victims of leprosy in some way or another.
• Care of the Elderly & Hospice care	This category should include projects supporting the care of the elderly and of terminally sick individuals aiming to provide comfort and promoting a better quality of life to individuals.
• Support to individuals with special needs	This category should identify projects aiming to ameliorate the lives and wellbeing of those individuals with special needs, including those with physical deformities or mental health issues.
• Medical Aid	This category should include projects supporting medical aid provisions or specialized equipment to institutions or individuals. It can also include actual medical service volunteer work done in the community.
• Child & family welfare support	This category should include projects targeting child and family welfare support projects. This may include support for orphanages and institutions caring for child welfare, and projects aiming to improve the lives of families in the community.
• Community support	This category should include projects aimed to support the community in general or sections of the community. Examples may include providing support for combatting drug abuse, supporting rape victims, food campaigns, shelter for the homeless, etc.
• Emergency Relief programs	This category should include projects that aim to support individuals or communities exposed to a natural or man-made disaster.

• Educational initiatives	This category should include support to promote education. This may involve bursaries to support individuals to follow educational targets or monetary or in-kind donations to assist educational establishments.
• Miscellaneous	This category should include any other charitable or philanthropic activity not covered by the preceding categories.

Each activity should be described in a standard format using the form overleaf. It is of course essential that all jurisdictions send their annual reports in time preferably by the end of March of the subsequent year. This will allow for timely publication and distribution of the report.

"In the same way, let your light shine before others, so that they may see your good works and give glory to your Father who is in heaven."

Matthew 5:16

CHARITABLE DONATION 1
fill a form for every charitable event (link photos)

Name of Beneficiary charity: *Wohltätigkeitsorganisation:* *Organisation caritative bénéficiaire:* *Organización benéfica beneficiaria:*	
Description of the charity: *Beschreibung der Wohltätigkeit:* *Description de charité:* *Descripción de la caridad:*	***NOT MORE THAN 250* words**
Activity of charity: *Wohltätigkeitsaktivität:* *Activité de charité:* *Actividad de caridad:*	Choose one: ☐ Leprosy-related programs ☐ Care of the Elderly & Hospice care ☐ Support to individuals with special needs ☐ Medical Aid ☐ Child & family welfare support ☐ Community support ☐ Emergency Relief programs ☐ Educational initiatives ☐ Miscellaneous - other
Country serviced: *Land gewartet:* *Pays desservi:* *País atendido:*	
Monetary Donations made: *Geldspenden gemacht:* *Dons monétaires effectués:* *Donaciones monetarias realizadas:*	
Goods Donations made: *Waren Spenden gemacht:* *Dons de marchandises effectués:* *Donaciones de bienes realizadas:*	
Volunteer hours utilized: *Freiwilligenstunden genutzt:* *Heures de bénévolat utilisées:* *Horas de voluntariado utilizadas:*	

Put any related photographs here

LAZARUS Hilfswerk (LHW)

 The LAZARUS Hilfswerk was founded in 1971-72 as a voluntary organization of the European Humanitarian Grand Priory. Its founding statute states: *In a society that is primarily based on the principle of performance, the old, disabled and sick person is often an outsider. This fact is the reason for us to mention the historical tasks and goals of the Military and Hospitaller Order of Saint Lazarus of Jerusalem LAZARUS Order, in a form adapted to the current conditions, for the benefit of the socially disadvantaged who need humanitarian aid.* In recognition of the successful work of the relief organization, the Grand Magisterium of the Order decided to integrate the relief organization institutionally into the overall international structure by setting up the independent jurisdiction 'Humanitarian Grand Priory Europe (Lazarus Relief Organization)' by Grand Master's decree, to which all LHW founding members now belong. The organization is based in Cologne, Germany. [60]

LAZARUS Hilfswerk began its existence with the implementation of disabled transport services in Cologne, Düsseldorf and Euskirchen, and later extended the service in other federal states. It now further operates facilities for elderly care and day-care centres. Other fields of services include outpatient care services, meals-on-wheels, construction, and

---

[60] LAZARUS Hilfswerk. Wikipedia – the free encyclopaedia. Wikimedia Foundation Inc., 2022, available at https://de.wikipedia.org/wiki/Lazarus_Hilfswerk

operation of facilities for assisted living with Senior citizens' clubs and nursing homes (St. Lazarus houses), and also social-educational family and youth welfare measures. In the 1990s, the LHW opened its first inpatient care facilities (St. Lazarus houses in Krefeld-Hüls and Wuppertal), and other houses followed. About 700 persons are employed by the organization today. Since its foundation, the LHW has been a recognized employment centre for the federal voluntary service.

In the early 1980s, the focus of work was expanded to include international humanitarian aid abroad and additional outpatient services. As part of the international humanitarian aid, LAZARUS Hilfswerk initiated the establishment of social institutions (training centres for social professions, social centres, and transport services for the disabled, meals-on-wheels and soup kitchens) in countries of the former Eastern bloc. In Poland, a close cooperation was established with the Charity Commission of the Polish Bishops' Conference (Komisja Caritatywna Episkopatu Polski - KCEP). To this day, LHW and the Humanitarian Grand Priory Europe of the Order of Lazarus support the further expansion of the network of Lazarus social stations in Warmia Masuria, outpatient home nursing and outpatient hospice services. Institutional cooperation with the German-Polish Working Group on Local Political Partnership (AKP) promotes these expansion plans.

The humanitarian work of the Humanitarian Grand Priory Europe (GPEU) is today carried out by several registered LAZARUS sub-organizations, which are delimited from one another owing to legal regulations and organizational requirements. Thus, professional, social, humanitarian and youth care activities required the establishment of sub-organizations each with its own legal personality. This was a basic requirement to enable contracts and agreements to be made as an official NGO within the European Community, the Federal Foreign Office and with social authorities. In this context, it is important that the employees of the Lazarus organizations have special professional qualifications depending on the job. Thus, besides acting independently, the Humanitarian Grand Priory Europe acts through the following LAZARUS sub-organizations:

- **LAZARUS Hilfswerk in Deutschland e.V.** manages a total of five inpatient care facilities. Throughout 2019 the largest inpatient facility - **LAZARUS Haus Wuppertal** - cared for a total of 144 residents. The occupancy rate was 96.6%. Additionally, the institution has the facility of eleven assisted-living serviced apartments, in which 14 senior citizens were able to lead an independent life during the course of the year. Another inpatient care facility - **LAZARUS Haus Cologne** - cared for a total of 100 residents who made use of the facility. The occupancy rate was 95.7%. The LAZARUS Hilfswerk in Deutschland e.V. also manages three centres providing Outpatient Care Services to support people in need and their relatives with care at home. In 2019 the centre located in Frechen-Bergheim employed 17 nurses who cared for a total of 107 clients; the centre located in Hürth employed 17 nurses caring for 66 clients; and the centre in Krefeld employed 22 nurses caring for 117 clients. The services at Hürth also offer the facility of a shared apartment for people with dementia, providing them with around-the-clock care. Nine senior citizens made use of this facility.

LAZARUS Haus Wuppertal

LAZARUS Haus Cologne

- **LAZARUS Betriebsführungs und Trägergeselsschaft Gemeinnützige GmbH** provides a semi-inpatient care facility with day-care and single-room facilities for living with all the amenities that the residents require. During 2019 the facility employed 54 nurses who looked after a total of 94 residents. The occupancy rate was 90.5%. The day-care provision cares for 38 guests during the year. Work is underway to expand the facilities to Heerstrasse.

LAZARUS Haus Heerstrasse

- **LAZARUS Niederrrhein Gemeinnützig GmbH** provides the services of two inpatient care facilities in the geriatric care sector: a semi-inpatient care facility accommodating 36 persons with day-care offers and a residential facility with service. The Kempen facility looked after 40 resident senior citizens in the course of

2019. The occupancy rate was 99.7%. In addition, the Kempen facility cared for 38 day-care guests. The facility in Krefeld cared for 20 residents. The occupancy rate was 92.4%. The facility also has 45 access-facilitated apartments which, during 2019, were inhabited by 35 senior citizens.

LAZARUS Haus Kempen

LAZARUS Haus Krefeld

- **LAZARUS Jugend Gmeinnützige GmbH** provides day-care centres for young children. During 2019 the day-care centre **Kita am Turm** in Bergheim catered for 46 children, while the day-care centre in Bornheim-Merten catered for 55 children. The day-care centre **Lazarus Kita Kerpen** catered for up to 50 children.

LAZARUS Haus Bergheim

- **LAZARUS Warmia I Mazury Welfare Centres** – The Elblag/Elbing Branch caters to individuals suffering from disabilities and handicaps, poverty and illness, joblessness, or social marginalization. During 2019, 418 people were supported, accounting for an average of 330 persons per month. The training program involved a total of 96,700 hours, an average of 8,064 hours per month. A subsidy of PLN 1,838,696.00 [€412,575] was received from the Elbląg Town Hall.

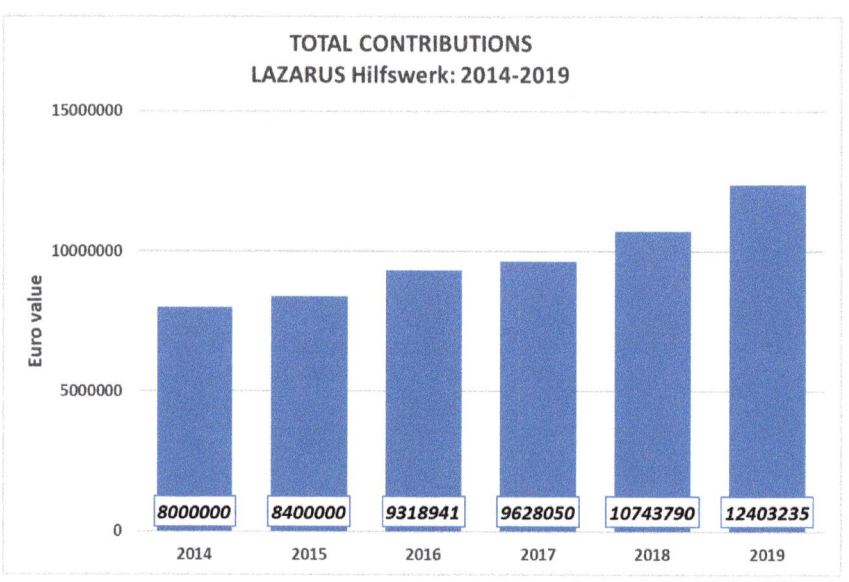

International Hospitaller Projects

During the Grand Magistral Council meeting held in Helsinki on the 7-8th September 1982, the Grand Hospitallers enquired about potential interest among the twenty-seven extant jurisdictions regarding a major joint project *which would bring worldwide recognition to the Order of Saint Lazarus.*[61] Three potential Grand Hospitaller flagship projects were then proposed:

a) Setting up an annually or biennial award in the field of medicine given to an individual who has made a significant scientific contribution under difficult circumstances. Proposed by the Grand Priory of Finland/Sweden, this proposal was deemed as *feasible and promising, with a modest effort.* It does not however appear to have been taken up on an international level.[62]

b) Supporting the setting up of a hospital in Malta under the name of Saint Lazarus of Jerusalem administered by the Maltese government and regular local staff supplemented by volunteer physicians from the Order. This proposal, put forward by the Grand Priory of Germany, was considered as *difficult for political*

---

[61] MHOSLJ. The Military and Hospitaller Order of Saint Lazarus of Jerusalem - Report of the Magistral Council held in Helsinki, Finland 7th-8th September 1982. MHOSLJ, 1982, +74pp.

[62] The Grand Priory of America had in 1975 instituted the ALAN WEAVER HAZELTON AWARD which was presented to individuals who by their activity within the Order, and by example of their lives, stands out in the traditions and ideals of loyalty, service and devotion to the Order. The award consisted of a hand-carved statuette of Saint Lazarus.

and financial reasons, particularly in view of the serious disagreements between the present Maltese government and the medical profession. The medical healthcare system in Malta at the time was being plagued by an ongoing industrial action strike initiated by the union for medical practitioners in 1977.

c) Setting up a program of support for Christians in the Holy Land. Proposed by the Grand Priory of America, this proposal was deemed as doable *with the cooperation of His Beatitude Patriarch Maximox V Hakin, and with the dedicated support of all members.* It could also *move the Order of Saint Lazarus into the forefront of the twentieth century.*

No action was taken towards implementing any of these proposals. During the Grand Magistral Council meeting held in Washington on the 12-15th July 1984, the Chancellor proposed that no decision should be taken regarding the institution of a St. Lazarus Prize for Medicine during that meeting, but that *all jurisdictions should in due course be asked to submit their reactions.* That meeting did however report on the work of the Lazarus-Volunteer Germany activities, especially the Polish Relief Project, whereby about 5.3 million kg of food with a value of about 16 million DM have been delivered up to July 1984. This support was very positively commented upon by Pope Paul John II who in 1983 commented: *"I thank you and all Volunteer and doners for all the good actions you did in the past especially for my native country and the good actions you did even in Germany for the welfare of the needy, sick and disabled and for all that what you will do in the future.*"[63] This charitable organization, founded in 1973, still serves as a jurisdictional showpiece of the hospitaller work being carried out by the German and Polish branches of the Order. In 2020, the Polish-based organization LAZARUS Ermland-Maßuren gave a monetary donation amounting to €451,941 and a total of 6,964 volunteer man-hours. The German-based organization LAZARUS Hilfswerk in Deutschland e.V further made a monetary donation of €11,069,000. This charitable work made up about 80% of the total hospitaller contribution made by the International Order during the year.[64]

The idea of having a joint project managed under the aegis of the Order to serve as the showcase of the Order's international philanthropic activities had long been a desideratum. In the latter part of the 1960s, with the support of the Maltese jurisdiction and the Grand Bailiff General and Commissioner General of the Order Lt. Col. Robert Gayre, an attempt was made by the Order to take over the management of a recently vacated hospital in Malta and set this up as a dedicated hospital of the Order. This project unfortunately fell through after the Malta Government decided to use the edifice to provide convalescent, oncology and dermatology

[63] MHOSLJ. The Military and Hospitaller Order of Saint Lazarus of Jerusalem - Report of the Magistral Council held in Washington, D.C., USA 12th to 15th July 1984. MHOSLJ, 1984, p.78, 67-77.
[64] Savona-Ventura, Charles. The Military and Hospitaller Order of St. Lazarus of Jerusalem. International 2020 Hospitaller Report. MHOSLJ, 2021.

services.[65] After this ambitious initiative failed, a different approach to setting up a hospital suitable for recuperative patients was initiated. During the 1973 Chapter General, it was reported that *the Grand Commander announced the gift to the Order of Lochore House, with five flats, next to Villa Lochore. The method of handing over the property would be left to Notary Dr. J. Grech CLJ and Mr. Harold Farrugia OLJ to work out the best interest of the Order.* The original plan was to use these five flats as places for recuperation after illness, etc, by members of the Order and other recommended persons. The property was to be rented at a nominal rent of about £1 per annum while the occupiers would pay a nominal charge of £10 deposit and £10 monthly. The broad plan was to set up similar houses all over the world.[66] The Malta Recuperative Facility Project however never saw the light of day.[67]

During the 2001 Grand Magistral Council Meeting, the then Grand Hospitaller Chev. Dr. Moritsugu apparently attempted to encourage the jurisdictions to undertake an Organ Donation Awareness Programme on the lines that the Grand Priory of America had developed in the U.S.A. During that meeting, in the spirit of cooperation, the participants received

---

[65] Savona-Ventura, Charles. King George V Hospital in Malta – Sacra Infermeria for the Order of St. Lazarus of Jerusalem. Malta Medical Journal, 2015, 27(1):pp.53-56.

[66] MHOSLJ. The Military and Hospitaller Order of Saint Lazarus of Jerusalem - Inauguration of the Grand Chancery, Malta; Report of the Chapter General held on 11th and 12th May 1973 - Continuation of list of members, amendments to list of members. MHOSLJ, 1973, p.5; Letter from LtCol. Robert Gayre to various interested individuals – Subject 114, The Strand, Gzira dated 28th April 1973. Torri ta' Lanzun MHOSLJ Archives, Malta.

[67] MHOSLJ. Report of the Grand Magistral Council held in Liege, 3rd and 4th June 1972 - Continuation of List of Members, Amendments, and Audited Account. MHOSLJ, Malta, 1972, +24pp.

the 'green ribbon' representing Organ Donation.[68] This project in the U.S.A. is still ongoing, though not as a Flagship Project of the International Order. In 2004, the Lazarus Relief Organization - LAZARUS Hilfswerk, with the support of the International Order, successfully helped with several construction projects, particularly on the island of Nias in Indonesia following the devastating destruction of the tsunami that hit the region on 26th December 2003.

The concept of having joint projects as so-called Flagship Projects was revived in 2011. The Flagship Project was originally envisaged as a rallying charity for the whole Order on an international level to identify a particular charity that all jurisdictions can support. The charity is chosen by a majority decision made by all the jurisdictions. Financial support for these Flagship Projects was to be obtained through an annual voluntary donation of €5 by all the members of the Order worldwide.[69] The Grand Hospitaller reported that the identified Flagship projects would include:

- The continuous support of the 'Gandhiji Seva Niketan' Leprosy Surgery Centre of Dr Rémy Rousselot in Bhubaneswar, India; and

- The envisaged support for the Saint Louis Hospital in Jerusalem, erected on the foundations of the first leprosarium of the Order in the Holy Land.[70]

---

[68] Saint Lazarus Newsletter, November 2001, 19:p6.

[69] Mittelstaedt, Axel. The Military and Hospitaller Order of St. Lazarus of Jerusalem. International 2013 Hospitaller Report. MHOSLJ, 2014, p.12, 17.

[70] Mittelstaedt, Axel. The Military and Hospitaller Order of St. Lazarus of Jerusalem. International 2012 Hospitaller Report. MHOSLJ, 2013, pp.8-13.

Other hospitaller projects subsequently proposed and approved by the national jurisdictions included:

- 2020: Support for St Anne School in Rayak, Bekaa Valley, Lebanon, on the border with Syria. The school is managed by the Melkite Greek Catholic Church. From the accumulated Hospitaller Fund, a donation amounting to a total of €15,000 had been put aside supplemented by further donations totalling €4,000 forwarded by Finland and Norway. However, following the devastating effect of the explosion in Beirut on 4th August 2020, a decision was made to transfer the voted funds to support the Melkite Patriarchy's efforts to restore and rebuild the buildings of the Melkite Patriarchate School destroyed by the disastrous explosion in Beirut.

- April 2020: At a request from Dr José Enrique Alés Martínez, Head of Management and Research of Medical Oncology, and the recommendation of the Grand Master, the Hospitaller Fund supported the Ávila Healthcare Complex in Spain with a monetary donation of €10,000 to help the centre obtain essential rapid diagnostic tests, respirator consumables, and PPE gowns during the Covid-19 pandemic. A supplementary sum of €10,976 was paid by the Order using general funds. The Grand Master further advised that an appropriate Flagship Project for 2020-2021 should target COVID-19 relief efforts.

- In 2022, two Flagship projects targeted Emergency Relief provisions following the Tonga volcanic eruption and tsunami in January initiated by the Grand Priory of New Zealand [donation of €10,000], and the Ukrainian Refugee Support Initiative managed by the Grand Bailiwick of the Czech Republic following the Russian invasion in February [donation of €3,000]. The jurisdictions were encouraged also to make further direct donations to this project and to a similar relief support project managed by the European Humanitarian Grand Priory

In 2016, the proposal to institute a humanitarian award was again brought up for discussion. The setting up of a *St Lazarus International Humanitarian Prize* was proposed with '*the objective of recognising outstanding contributions to the spiritual and physical welfare of society, especially in times of emergency*'. The annual award would consist of a silver medal and a cash prize of €5,000. The proposed medal design to be adopted was proposed: '*Obverse – an allegorical scene of the raising of Lazarus; Reverse – the Arms of the Order with the motto "For Humanity" (or similar words) and a space to engrave the recipient's name, the object to be housed in a presentation box*'. The project was noted as being non-urgent and shelved for future discussion.[71] Unfortunately, the Covid-19 pandemic which started at the end of 2019 and is still ongoing, prevented physical meetings of the Grand Magistral Council and no definite decision has yet been made as to whether the introduction of the award will be taken up.

---

[71] Delahunt, Brett. Grand Hospitaller – Addendum – St Lazarus International Humanitarian Prize. GMC Agenda Item 8c(i) dated 18th November 2016, +1p.; Draft Minutes of the meeting of the Grand Magistral Council held on 3rd November 2018 in Madrid, Spain, item 10.3.

The Military and Hospitaller Order of Saint Lazarus of Jerusalem
Grand Master: His Excellency, Don Carlos Gereda y de Borbón, Marqués de Almazán

GRAND HOSPITALLER

Addendum

ST LAZARUS INTERNATIONAL HUMANITARIAN PRIZE

The St Lazarus International Humanitarian Prize has been established by The Military and Hospitaller Order of St Lazarus with the objective of recognizing outstanding contributions to the spiritual and physical welfare of society, especially in times of emergency.

The Award shall take the form of a silver medal and a cash prize of 5000 Euros.
The Prize may be awarded to individuals or organizations.

There shall be one award of the Prize in any year; however, the Order reserves the right to withhold the award of the Prize in any year if, in its opinion, no suitable candidate has been nominated.

Nominations for the St Lazarus International Humanitarian Prize shall be called for annually, with the closing date of December 17, this being the Feast Day of Saint Lazarus.

Nominations shall be in the form of confidential letter to the Grand Chancellor of The Order of St Lazarus. The nominating letter must include the curriculum vitae of the nominee. It must also provide detailed evidence as to the reasons the nominee should be considered for the award of the Prize. The nomination should also include supporting documentation from at least two referees.

Nominations for the St Lazarus International Humanitarian Prize shall be considered by a Committee of The Order consisting of the Ecclesiastical Grand Prior, the Grand Hospitaller and other members appointed by The Grand Master.

The Award shall be presented by The Grand Master at an international meeting of The Order or on some other appropriate occasion.

Brett Delahunt ONZM GCLJ MD FRCPA FRSNZ
Grand Hospitaller

1

King George V Hospital in Malta

Sacra Infermeria for the Order of St. Lazarus of Jerusalem

Introduction

King George V Seamen's Memorial Hospital sited in Floriana just outside the fortifications of Valletta in Malta was originally inaugurated on the 30th November 1922 to serve as memorial to the men of the Merchant Navy who died in the First World War.[72] The hospital was very severely damaged in April 1942 by enemy action during the Second World War and was subsequently reconstructed and inaugurated on the 30th November 1948. The hospital catered for sick and injured seamen of all nationalities and many dependents of the service personnel. Maltese patients were admitted when beds were available. In the early 1960s, financial constraints were being felt, though the managing trust – the Seaman's Christian Friend Society Hospital Trust – resisted the closure of the hospital in Malta since it was believed that it still had a functional role within the health care delivery system in Malta. However, in 1966, despite efforts to find financial support to maintain the hospital, the Trust decided that the hospital would have to be closed down or to be transferred to the Malta Government. It formally closed down its services on the 31st January 1967.[73]

---

[72] The Times [of Malta], 12th September 1918; The opening of King George V Merchant Seamen's Memorial Hospital, Malta. Daily Malta Chronicle, 30th November 1922.

[73] Letter from the Governor General Sir Maurice Dorman to Lt. Col. J.V. Abela OBE dated 19th July 1967 with several enclosures. Torri ta' Lanzun MHOSLJ Archives, Malta.

King George V Seaman's Memorial Hospital

The Order of St Lazarus interest

The Commandery of Malta of the Military and Hospitaller Order of Saint Lazarus of Jerusalem was set up with ten founder members on the 30th September 1966.[74] During the third council meeting of the new jurisdiction, on the 18th May 1967, it was suggested that the Commandery should endeavour to interest a number of industrialists to finance the running of the hospital under the auspices of the Order. Should the financial outlay outstrip the resources of the Commandery, an alternative proposal was to run the establishment as a clinic. An investigative commission was set up to make representations to the Governor General

---

[74] Savona-Ventura C. The Grand Priory of the Maltese Islands of the Military & Hospitaller Order of Saint Lazarus of Jerusalem – A historical review. Grand Priory – MHOSLJ, Malta, 2013.

meeting the Governor General on the 19th June.[75] The proposed suggestion that the management of KGV Hospital would to be taken over by the Order of St Lazarus was warmly received. The outcome of the meeting was subsequently reported to Lt. Col. Robert Gayre Grand Bailiff General and Commissioner General of the Order wherein a request was made for the support of other jurisdictions and individual members of the Order.[76]

A further meeting was held by the Hospitaller Commission of the Commandery of Malta with the Governor General with Lt. Col. Gayre and J.A. Maitland in attendance. On the 9th August 1967, Lt. Col. Gayre made several proposals as to future required actions, including the setting up by the Commandery of Malta of a Hospitaller Commission which would eventually serve as the Board of Directors for the Hospital and a Management Committee which would be eventually responsible to the day-to-day running of the hospital. A Board of Trustees would be responsible for the hospital funds. The latter was to be made up of the Grand Master of the Order, the Commissioner-General, the Grand Bailiffs of England and Scotland, the Grand Administrator of the Order, and further members nominated by the Commandery of Malta, the Governor General, the Malta Minister of Health, and the Scottish Red Cross. The scheduled timeline was to finalise discussion by September 1967, with a view of the Order

---

[75] Minutes of the Third Council Meeting of the Commandery of Malta dated 18th May 1967. Minutes of an Unofficial Meeting held on the 13th June 1967. Grand Priory – MHOSLJ Archives, Malta.

[76] Letter from Sir Hannibal P. Scicluna to Lt. Col. Gayre dated 20th June 1967. Torri ta' Lanzun MHOSLJ Archives, Malta; Letter from the Governor General …..dated 19th July 1967. Torri ta' Lanzun MHOSLJ Archives, Malta.

assuming control of the hospital by the 1st January 1968 and opening a functional hospital by March 1968. The proposed funding was to come through the adoption of beds by various jurisdictions of the Order, the business community of Malta, paying patients, private trusts such as the Nuffield Foundation, and the British Government.[77]

Representations were then made to the Malta Government. While the Malta Minister of Health was interested in the proposal and the offer to use the Order's contacts and influence with the original Seaman's Christian Friend Society Hospital Trust, he appeared reluctant to commit the Government as to what part the Order would play in the management of the reopened hospital. Lt. Col. Gayre requested a Letter of Intent from the Government of Malta to be in a legally viable position to open negotiations with the original Trust.[78] The apparent impasse was discussed by the Council of the Commandery of Malta on the 28th September. During that meeting, it was reported that the archbishop had been informed and had given his approval for the Order's plans for KGV Hospital. During the subsequent Council Meeting of 9th November, Lt. Col. Gayre informed the Council that while the Order as a whole was ready to finance the running of the hospital, the Minister of Health had given a negative reply to the request for the Letter of Intent necessary for the Order to start

---

[77] Letter from Lt. Col. Gayre to Mr J. Amato Gauci dated 9th August 1967. Torri ta' Lanzun MHOSLJ Archives, Malta.

[78] Letter from Ms. A. Morrison Private secretary to the Grand Bailiff General to Mr. J. Amato Gauci Private Secretary to H.E. Governor General dated 28th August 1967. Letter from Ms. A. Morrison to Mr J. Amato Gauci dated 12th October 1967. Torri ta' Lanzun MHOSLJ Archives, Malta.

negotiations.[79] KGV Hospital reverted to the Malta Government on the 27th November 1967.[80]

Despite a number of representations made to the Governor-General and the Minister of Health by representatives of the Order, no progress was registered in obtaining a Letter of Intent from the Malta Government. At the Council Meeting of the Commandery of Malta on the 10th October 1968, a decision was made for a delegation to visit the Minister of Health. The meeting was held on the 21st October 1968. During this meeting, the Minister asked for a formal request from the Order to take over KGV Hospital clearly stating the purpose the hospital will be used for and who will be the intended beneficiaries. The Order was to provide proof of having sufficient funds to support the necessary restorations needed. It appeared that other organizations had shown an interest in acquiring the hospital as well. This formal application was sent to the Minister of Health on the 2nd November 1968.[81] No response was forthcoming from the Government to the formal application. During the Council Meeting of the Commandery of Malta on the 6th February 1969, the general impression obtained after informal talks with the Secretary to

---

[79] Minutes of the Fourth Council Meeting of the Commandery of Malta dated 28th September 1967. Minutes of the Fifth Council Meeting of the Commandery of Malta dated 9th November 1967. Grand Priory – MHOSLJ Archives, Malta.

[80] PQ 3849: Hon. K. Agius MP to Hon. Minister of Health. Torri ta' Lanzun MHOSLJ Archives, Malta

[81] Minutes of the Ninth Council Meeting of the Commandery of Malta dated 21st October 1968. Grand Priory – MHOSLJ Archives, Malta; Letter from J.V. Abela to Lt. Col. Gayre dated 21st October 1968. Letter signed by members of the Commandery of Malta to Hon. Dr. Alexander Cachia Zammit Minister of Health dated 2nd November 1968. Torri ta' Lanzun MHOSLJ Archives, Malta.

the Minister of Health was that the Order's application to take over the management of KGV Hospital had little chance of being considered. It was opinioned that the Sovereign Military Order of Malta may have also shown as interest in acquiring the property.[82] A request was made to the Medical Officer-in-charge, Royal Naval Hospital in Malta Surgeon Rear-Admiral Dudley P. Gurd who was a member of the Order of St. Lazarus (GC No. 0129) to approach the Minister of Health to stress the continuing interest of the Order in acquiring KGV Hospital. Failing this, the Order would withdraw its formal application.[83] Rear Admiral Gurd met with the Minister of Health Dr. Cachia Zammit on the 21st February 1969. He was reassured that the Government was still positively disposed towards the application made by the Order of St. Lazarus though there were still some reservations that needed to be ironed out. The proposal had to be submitted to the Government Cabinet who had to decide whether the Malta Government was to assume full responsibility for KGV Hospital or devolve the responsibility to a managing organization. The report of that meeting was presented to the Council of the Commandery of Malta on the 5th March 1969 and forwarded to the Minister of Health on 7th March 1969.[84] During that Council Meeting, Col. J.V. Abela informed the members that Barclays Bank was prepared to authorize an advance of

---

[82] Minutes of the Tenth Council Meeting of the Commandery of Malta dated 6th February 1969. Grand Priory-MHOSLJ Archives, Malta.

[83] Minutes of the Tenth Council Meeting …. 6th February 1969. Grand Priory-MHOSLJ Archives, Malta.

[84] Report of a meeting between Rear Admiral D.P. Gurd and the Hon. Minister of Health Dr. Cachia Zammit held on the 21st February 1969 presented to the Council of the Commandery of Malta on the 5th March 1969 and forwarded to the Minister of Health on 7th March 1969. Torri ta' Lanzun MHOSLJ Archives, Malta.

£10,000 – 25,000 provided suitable guarantors were available. It was stated that to date the Grand Master was ready to guarantee £500, Lt. Col. Gayre £1,000, Chev. Zammit £50 and Col. Abela £500.[85] Further guarantors were to be found to make available the necessary funds. In the subsequent days, other members of the Commandery of Malta accepted to serve as guarantors: Prof. Canon C. Muscat £100; and Anthony Miceli Farrugia £1,000.[86] Dr Cachia Zammit eventually denied ever having received any offer by the Order of St. Lazarus to manage King George V Hospital.[87] On the 31st May 1969, the Malta Government announced that a decision had been made to take over the management of KGV Hospital.[88] On the 6th June 1969, the Commandery of Malta representing the Order informed the Minister of Health that the Order was withdrawing its offer to assume the management of King George V Hospital.[89]

Conclusion

The hospital renamed Sir Paul Boffa Hospital reopened in December 1970 under the management of the Department of Health to form part of the national healthcare serviced provision system providing convalescent, oncology, and dermatology & venerology services.

---

[85] Minutes of the Eleventh Council Meeting of the Commandery of Malta dated 5th March 1969. Grand Priory – MHOSLJ Archives, Malta; Circular No. 4/69 to members of the Commandery of Malta and subsequent response letters. Torri ta' Lanzun MHOSLJ Archives, Malta.

[86] Circular No. 4/69. Grand Priory-MHOSLJ Archives, Malta.

[87] Parliamentary Question No. 5318 dated 7th April 1969. Torri ta' Lanzun MHOSLJ Archives, Malta.

[88] Il-Haddiem, 31st May 1969.

[89] Letter from J. Amato Gauci Commandery secretary to Hon. Dr. A. Cachia Zammit Minister of Health dated 4th June 1969. Torri ta' Lanzun MHOSLJ Archives, Malta.

'Gandhiji Seva Niketan' Leprosy Surgery Centre

The 'Gandhiji Seva Niketan' Leprosy Surgery Centre support project was undertaken in 2011 through a collaborative effort of the Grand Priory of Romania, the Grand Bailiwick of Germany, the Grand Priory of England and Wales, the Hilfswerk Deutscher Zahnarzte, and the Commandery of Wallendorf under the direction of the Grand Hospitaller. The project aimed to  support the work done by Dr. Remy l. Rousselot and his team. From July 1986 to December 2011, 10,870 operations had been performed on 6,375 victims of leprosy at the centre. Support from the Order continued in subsequent year.[90] In 2014, a total of €9,200 was provided in support of the work done by the Centre by various jurisdictions of the Order. During that year, the Centre performed 637 operations serving leprosy patients from the two large leprosy colonies in Cuttack and five leprosy colonies of the State Capital Bhubaneswar and the thirty districts of Odisha. [91]

---

[90] Mittelstaedt, Axel. The Military and Hospitaller Order of St. Lazarus of Jerusalem. International 2012 Hospitaller Report. MHOSLJ, 2013

[91] Mittelstaedt, Axel. The Military and Hospitaller Order of St. Lazarus of Jerusalem. International 2013 Hospitaller Report. MHOSLJ, 2014

https://www.facebook.com/vision.teilen/photos

The support is ongoing being maintained by individual national jurisdictions. In 2020, the Grand Bailiwick of Germany and the Bavarian sub-jurisdiction made a monetary donation of €26,530 towards the workings of the 50-bed Centre. During 2020, the clinic carried out around 550 operations including amputations. It also serves the needs of victims of Hansen's Disease in the community by providing an outpatient service.[92]

---

[92] Savona-Ventura, Charles. The Military and Hospitaller Order of St. Lazarus of Jerusalem. International 2020 Hospitaller Report. MHOSLJ, 2021

GANDHIJI SEVA NIKETAN
- Joseph Bahadur Memorial Foundation -
Plot No. 762, Jayadev Vihar
Bhubaneswar
751 013, ORISSA
INDIA

GANDHIJI SEVA NIKETAN
LEPROSY SURG. CENTRE
550, DUMUDUMA
BHUBANESWAR
ODISHA-751019

Statistical Report of the Medico-surgical activities in favour of the destitute

Handicapped Leprosy Patients of Odisha up to 31st December 2011.

LEPROSY SURGERY in all its aspects remains the essential part of our activities:

From July 1986 till end of December 2011, 10.870 operations on 6375 Leprosy Patients have been performed in Odisha by Dr. Remy L.R., MD, and his team.

During the years 1986-1994, the surgical operations were performed exclusively at "Gandhiji Shanti Nivas"- Janla, in the district of Khurda.

From the year 1995 onwards, the surgery was expanded to benefit also to other leprosy Centres, thanks to the creation of the medical voluntary organization (N.G.O.) "GANDHIJI SEVA NIKETAN".

Hence, during the year 1995, the first surgical mobile unit of our registered Society "GANDHIJI SEVA NIKETAN" was created at "Shanti Ashram", Nayabazar, Cuttack, to cater to the needs of the leprosy patients of the two leprosy colonies of "Gandhipalli" and "Nehrupalli".

Thereafter, "GANDHIJI SEVA NIKETAN" took steps to operate its main own surgical centre for handicapped at DUMUDUMA, near Khandagiri in the outskirts of Bhubaneswar, where the surgical complex of "GANDHIJI SEVA NIKETAN"-Dumuduma was inaugurated by the District Authorities in August 1997, and became operational on 15th October 1997 onwards. It has presently a capacity of 50 surgical beds with all the attached facilities such as Operation Theater with electrical incinerator for safe disposal of surgical wastes, as well as solar equipment. This Leprosy surgical Centre offers FREE service for surgery to the Leprosy patients in need. **In fourteen years of activities at DUMUDUMA, 4.084 leprosy patients have been admitted** in this surgical centre, where the medical team of "Gandhiji Seva Niketan" **performed 6.837 operations** on their deformed hands and feet. The leprosy patients are coming from the districts of all over Odisha, as well as from the neighbouring States to seek admission at Dumuduma.

(See details in annexure).

- 1 -

Moreover, "GANDHIJI SEVA NIKETAN" has started in September 2003 a specific activity of PREVENTION of leprosy deformities for the 5 biggest leprosy colonies within Bhubaneswar Municipal Corporation: on the 10th of each month, the lected representatives of these 5 Leprosy colonies of Bhubaneswar are coming to our Leprosy Surgical Centre of Dumuduma to collect bandages' material for SELF-CARE of small minor wounds on their limbs, hands & feet, so that further major infections do not occur by lack of hygiene. We are distributing FREE OF COST:

- Rolled gauze bandages;
- Cotton wool;
- Dettol antiseptic lotion;
- Merbromin tincture;
- Antibiotic Soframycin Skin cream.

The five leprosy colonies getting the benefit of this free distribution of bandages' material are:

1/ "RAMA KRISHNA" Leprosy Colony, Unit III, Sriya Talkies, Bhubaneswar-1;

2/ "JAGANNATH" Leprosy Colony, Rasulgarh, Bhubaneswar-10;

3/ "LINGARAJ" Leprosy Colony, Old Town, Bhubaneswar-2;

4/ "GOKHI BABA" Leprosy Colony, Sunderpada, Bhubaneswar-2;

5/ "NETAJI SUBASH CHANDRA BOSE" Leprosy Colony, Vani Vihar, Bhubaneswar-6.

Around 420 Leprosy patients from these 5 Leprosy Colonies , all with plantar ulcers, are getting the benefit of this monthly free distribution of bandages' material by "GANDHIJI SEVA NIKETAN".

Bhubaneswar, 31st December 2011,

31-12-2011

Dr. Remy Luc ROUSSELOT.

GANDHIJI SEVA NIKETAN
LEPROSY SURG. CENTRE
550, DUMUDUMA
BHUBANESWAR
ODISHA-751019

Return to Jerusalem – The Saint Louis Hospital

Historical research revealed that the Crusader establishment of the order of Saint Lazarus outside the walls of Jerusalem was located just opposite to where the New Gate to the modern city lies. The area is presently occupied by Saint Louis Hospital French Catholic Congregation of the Sisters of Saint Joseph of the Apparition.

The modern establishment has 50 beds catering for patients in Palliative Care (Hospice) and Geriatric Hospitalization (Geriatric Home and Geriatric Ward for specialized nursing care). It is fully recognized by the Israeli Ministry of Health and the Israeli Social Insurance System. It is open and used by all religions. Because of increasing demands for its services and new healthcare service regulations imposed in 2011 by the Israeli government, the Congregation was obliged to update and augment its facilities. Financial assistance was being sought by the Congregation to support the renovations.

The Order of Saint Lazarus committed itself to assist in the complete renovation of the clinic kitchen, including the inventory which, after completion, will correspond to the European HACCP hygiene regulations (EN 14065). The Hazard Analysis and Critical Control Points (HACCP) concept is a preventive system designed to ensure both food safety and consumer safety. The renovated kitchen of this institution would also enable it to better cater to the meal choices of Jewish, Muslim and Christian patients alike. Moreover, it will ensure that any special diets required by patients' conditions can also be prepared.

The estimated renovation costs amounting to €174,000 including:

- Shell construction costs   €88,500
- Plumbing/electrical costs   €19,500
- Air conditioners   €17,000
- Costs for equipment   €62,500
- Planning costs   €8,500
- Contingency (3%)   €6,000
- Total cost   €174,000

The Congregation could itself afford to commit €20,000 for the project, thus the expected funding from the Order of Saint Lazarus was estimated to be in the order of €154,000.

On 2nd May 2014, the Chapter of the Grand Bailiwick of Germany – with the support guaranteed by the Stiftung Hilfswerk Deutscher Zahnärzte für Lepra- und Notgebiete [C.H.Bartels Fund] (German Dentists' Relief Organization and the Deutsche Lazarus Stiftung (German Lazarus Foundation) pledged the required amount, and also decided to transfer responsibility for safeguarding and submitting the project funds in organizational terms to the German Lazarus Foundation. The national jurisdictions of the Order were subsequently asked to contribute and make generous financial donations.

The solemn re-inauguration ceremony took place on the 19th June 2016. The head of the hospital, Sister Monika Düllmann of the Congregation of Saint Joseph of the Apparition, was able to welcome a great number of guests on the premises of the renovated hospital. The delegation of the Order of Saint Lazarus were guests of honour. A bronze commemorative plaque was mounted on the wall of the establishment.